D1260047

THE RENEWAL OF WORSHIP

P-21
P
F.C.

THE RENEWAL
OF
WORSHIP

ESSAYS BY MEMBERS
OF THE
JOINT LITURGICAL GROUP

Edited by
Ronald C. D. Jasper

London
OXFORD UNIVERSITY PRESS
NEW YORK   TORONTO
1965

Oxford University Press, Amen House, London E.C.4

GLASGOW NEW YORK TORONTO MELBOURNE WELLINGTON
BOMBAY CALCUTTA MADRAS KARACHI LAHORE DACCA
CAPE TOWN SALISBURY NAIROBI IBADAN ACCRA
KUALA LUMPUR HONG KONG

*Printed in Great Britain
by Western Printing Services Ltd.
Bristol*

CONTENTS

MEMBERS OF THE JOINT LITURGICAL GROUP

1. *Church of England*
   The Dean of Bristol (The Very Revd. D. E. W. Harrison, M.A.) *Chairman*
   The Bishop of Knaresborough (The Rt. Revd. H. de Candole, M.A.)
   The Revd. Canon R. C. D. Jasper, M.A., D.D., F.R.Hist.S. *Secretary*

2. *Church of Scotland*
   The Revd. J. A. Lamb, M.A., Ph.D., D.D.
   F. N. Davidson Kelly, Esq., LL.B., S.S.C.

3. *The Baptist Union of Great Britain and Ireland*
   The Revd. Neville Clark, M.A., S.T.M.
   The Revd. Stephen F. Winward, M.A., B.D.

4. *The Congregational Union of England and Wales*
   The Revd. J. M. Todd, M.A.
   The Revd. J. Huxtable, M.A.[1]

5. *The Episcopal Church in Scotland*
   The Bishop of Glasgow, Primus (The Most Revd. F. H. Moncrieff, M.A.)
   The Revd. Canon D. Nicholson, M.A.

6. *The Methodist Church*
   The Revd. Rupert E. Davies, M.A., B.D.
   The Revd. A. Raymond George, M.A., B.D.

7. *Presbyterian Church of England*
   The Revd. R. Aled Davies, M.A.
   The Revd. R. D. Whitehorn, M.A., D.D.

[1] Since contributing an essay to this Symposium, Mr. Huxtable has been appointed General Secretary of the Congregational Union and has resigned from the Group. The Revd. W. S. Evans has been appointed in his place.

STATEMENT

Informal discussion on liturgical matters between interested people from various Churches in Great Britain have indicated that the time is now ripe for the creation of a Joint Liturgical Group which can develop given projects and questions of public worship. The Archbishop of Canterbury was asked to help bring such a Group into being by issuing invitations to the Churches concerned to appoint members. His Grace kindly agreed to do so and himself appointed the representatives of the Church of England, while those of other Churches have been appointed by their respective bodies.

At its first meeting on 10–11 October 1963 the Group elected the Dean of Bristol as its Chairman and Dr. Jasper as its Secretary.

It is clearly to be understood that any work produced by this Group will have no authority greater than that which its own members give to it by their own weight; but it will be for particular Churches, through their own customary modes of decision, to make use of the results if they are willing to do so.

The initial projects which the Group has decided to discuss are these:

1. The planning of a Calendar, Forms of Daily Service, and a Lectionary which the Churches might be glad to have in common.
2. The planning of joint forms of service which might be used with the approval of the several Churches on occasions

for united worship, such as the Week of Prayer for Unity and Holy Week.
3. The consideration of the structure of the service of Holy Communion.

11 October 1963

THE RENEWAL OF WORSHIP: INTRODUCTION

R. C. D. JASPER

Among the many recent blessings of the ecumenical movement, one in particular is of decisive importance for the common mission of the churches in our time. It is the current 'rediscovery' of Christian worship—of that twofold 'service' to God and to the world which is expressed in the biblical term *leitourgia* (liturgy)— as the central, determinative act of the Church's life. There is no clearer evidence of this than the joint theological work produced since the last Faith and Order Conference at Lund in 1952, the growth of the Liturgical Movement in virtually all Christian traditions and the common recognition of an essential connection between the worship of the Church and its missionary task. It is heartening to realize that, at a time when Christians are perhaps more aware of the tragic estrangement of the world from the Church than ever before, God is so plainly calling us to rediscover together the joy, the depth and the power of Christian worship.

THIS statement, taken from the Report of the Fourth Section of the Faith and Order Conference at Montreal in the summer of 1963, expresses in brief compass the convictions underlying the creation of the Joint Liturgical Group: and this book of essays is an attempt to say something about these convictions and to indicate a few of the tasks which the Group hopes to undertake.

It has often been said that the origin of the Liturgical Movement can be traced to the revival of Benedictine

monasticism in France during the nineteenth century. In 1832
Dom Prosper Guéranger refounded the Benedictine abbey
of Solesmes and devoted his energies to the restoration of the
Gregorian chant and a rediscovery of the liturgical inheritance of the Church. He made mistakes; and subsequently his
work was subjected to considerable criticism, mainly on the
grounds of too great a reliance on the thought and practice of
the Middle Ages. But it was a pioneer work, initiating a new
interest in liturgy which later resulted in the brilliant studies
of such scholars as Batiffol, Cabrol and Connolly. Guéranger's
interests had also been academic, and it was not until the
election of Pope Pius X in 1903 that the movement became
more pastoral in character. Only three months after taking
office he issued a *Motu proprio* on church music encouraging
the more active participation of the faithful in the worship
of the Church. 'Since it is indeed Our most fervent wish that
the true Christian Spirit should flourish anew in every sphere
and be treasured by all the faithful, we must above all consider the sanctity and dignity of the house of God, for it is
there that the faithful meet to attain this spirit at its most
important and indispensable source, which is active participation in the most sacred mysteries and in the public and
solemn prayer of the Church.'[1] A further decree followed in
1905 urging more frequent communion and in 1911 and
1913 there were measures to reform the Calendar and the
Breviary. The spread of the movement was fostered mainly
by the Benedictines at Maria Laach in Germany under Abbot
Ildefons Herwegen and at Mont César, Louvain in Belgium
under Dom Lambert Beauduin. The latter, whose little book
La Piété de l'Église (1914) (*Liturgy, the Life of the Church*)
became a classical document, emphasized three great truths.
In the first place, a clear conception of the Incarnation would

[1] *Motu proprio* 'Tra le Sollecitudine', sc. 7, 22 November 1903.

result in a recognition of the dignity of human nature and the life of the world. Secondly, realization that the Church was the Body of Christ would bring a new sense of fellowship into life and worship. Thirdly, an acknowledgement of the sacrifice of Christ would result in men truly living the eucharistic sacrifice, offering with him the sacrifices which their Christian lives would bring. Fundamentally, worship was a joint undertaking of the people of God, involving them all in sharing the redemptive work of Christ in the world.

In recent decades the movement has gathered momentum in a remarkable and exciting way. In 1947 came the notable Papal Encyclical 'Mediator Dei et Hominum'—the first encyclical to be devoted entirely to the liturgy, and sometimes described as 'the Magna Carta of the Liturgical Movement': and in January 1964 appeared the *Motu proprio* on the Constitution of the Liturgy, setting out the lines on which the Roman liturgy is to be reformed in order to (1) 'impart an ever-increasing vigour to the Christian life of the faithful; (2) adapt more suitably to the needs of our age those institutions which are subject to change; (3) foster whatever can promote union among all who believe in Christ; (4) strengthen whatever can help to call all mankind into the Church's fold'.[1]

This is the barest outline of an interesting development: but it is a story which gives only part of the whole picture. The Liturgical Movement has not been confined entirely to the Roman Catholic Church. The Reformed Churches on the Continent have also had their pioneers. There was, for example, Jean Frederic Ostervald, pastor of Neuchâtel in Switzerland from 1683 to 1747, who produced what was really the first Reformed prayer book. He was in advance of

[1] 'The Constitution on the Sacred Liturgy', sc. 1.

his time in advocating truly congregational worship, the observance of the Christian calendar, and the use of primitive elements such as the Sursum Corda, the Sanctus and the Gloria in Excelsis in the Communion Service. Although Ostervald himself never moved from Neuchâtel, his work had wide significance, being adopted by Reformed congregations in America and influencing the liturgical revival in Scotland during the nineteenth century.

Rather more contemporary with Guéranger was Eugène Bersier, pastor of the French Reformed l'Église d'Étoile in Paris, who also saw the need for worship to be a corporate action. In 1876 he produced a new liturgy, emphasizing the centrality of the eucharist, the importance of the Christian calendar, and the need for holding Word and Sacrament in balance. While the French Reformed Church as a whole was not prepared to accept his ideas, his work was not wasted, for it proved to have a considerable influence on subsequent developments. Since his day, too, Lutheran and Reformed scholars such as Otto, Heiler, Brilioth and Cullmann have made contributions to liturgical study no less valuable than those of their Roman Catholic contemporaries; while a veritable spate of new liturgies has been produced, of which perhaps the most interesting is that of the French community at Taizé.

On this side of the Channel the story is similar. In the Church of England one can see in the second generation of Tractarians the precursors of the Liturgical Movement. Their emphasis on eucharistic worship went hand in hand with intense pastoral zeal, and the self-sacrificing labour of men like Charles Lowder in Wapping imprinted itself on the minds of their parishioners. 'They have learnt and proved that it is the most blessed privilege of our union with Christ to bear the Cross with Him, and sympathize in all the sufferings of His Body for His Church's sake. And in consequence they are the most united congregation I have ever met with. . . . It is an astonishing exception to the usual London congregation in the real family life which characterizes it.'[1] So wrote one of Lowder's curates. Admittedly these men made mistakes. Like Guéranger they were wrong in looking too much to the Middle Ages: but these 'Ritualists', as they were called, did a great deal to stimulate interest in both the liturgy and the mission of the Church. Men like W. J. Butler of Wantage and W. J. E. Bennett of Frome really stood four-square with the aims and ideals of the Parish and People Movement of today.

The nineteenth century also saw a renewed interest in liturgy in Scotland. In 1857 Dr. Robert Lee began to use his *Prayers for Public Worship* in the Kirk of the Greyfriars, Edinburgh. As with Bersier, his ideas by no means met with general approval; but he had started a movement which soon spread. Within a matter of months the Revd. Andrew Bonar, convinced of the need for a Scottish liturgy published anonymously his little book on *Presbyterian Liturgies*; while in 1865 the Church Service Society was formed, taking as its aim 'the study of the liturgies, ancient and modern, of the Christian Church, with a view to the preparation and ulti-mate publication of certain forms of prayer for public worship, and services for the administration of the sacra-ments'. Its *Euchologion*, published in 1867, was highly success-ful, enjoyed a long life and undoubtedly paved the way for the Church of Scotland's present books, *The Book of Common Order*, *The Ordinal and Service Book*, and *Prayers for the Christian Year*.

The Free Churches, too, have had their liturgical pioneers. Consider, for example, those distinguished ministers of the

---

[1] Anon, *Charles Lowder: A Biography* (1882), p. 165.

King's Weigh House Chapel, London—Dr. Thomas Binney (1798–1874) and Dr. John Hunter (1848–1917). Binney, it is claimed, 'changed the face of preaching, prayer and praise in Congregationalism'.[1] He believed that worship was the offering of the whole Church, congregation as well as minister: the people 'shall be called vocally to utter some portion of the Church's *common prayer*, so . . . that they shall feel that they positively *do* pray, as well as listening to another praying'.[2] Consequently he urged that there should be a combination of free prayer and set forms; and it was he who introduced into Free Church worship the chanting of the psalms and canticles. Hunter, like Binney, believed in corporate worship and his approach was truly ecumenical, claiming that 'it is time the Free Churches of England had outgrown their fear of everything Roman or Anglican'.[3] His *Devotional Services*, the 'first dignified Congregational Liturgy in English',[4] has had a profound influence on pastoral theology in the Free Churches. Nearer our own time another distinguished liturgical scholar, Dr. W. E. Orchard, has also been Minister of the King's Weigh House Chapel: it would therefore be true to say that this building has played a valuable part in the liturgical development of the Free Churches.

From such beginnings as these the Liturgical Movement has developed in all the Churches, and at the same time there have been notable developments in other fields—the Ecumenical Movement, biblical and sacramental theology, and sociology. But what has become most apparent is the growth of a spirit of healthy self-criticism—a desire for the Church to come to grips with itself and with the world. The Vatican Council is an example of this, for here we see the Church of Rome freeing itself—at a cost—from the rigidity which has

---

[1] Horton Davies, *Worship and Theology in England*, vol. iv (1962), p. 223.
[2] Ibid.   [3] Op. cit., p. 234.   [4] Op. cit., p. 230.

held it fast since the Counter-Reformation. The Reformed Churches, too, are increasingly ready to investigate their own traditions and judge them by external standards. Symptomatic of this is the recognition by the Church of England that the *Book of Common Prayer is* capable of improvement and is not *quite* so incomparable as she once would have men believe. And Christians everywhere are becoming increasingly aware that the Church of today resembles the Primitive Church in that it is not so much a large and powerful organization more or less coterminous with a whole nation as it is a small group, needing to shape its life and thought in a way that can not only make sense to its own members, but also have an impact on those outside it.

In the liturgical field this spirit of self-criticism has produced a remarkable growing together, indicated in the statement of Charles Davis, Professor of Dogmatic Theology at the Roman Catholic college of St. Edmund's, Ware.

One of the results of the Liturgical Movement has been to bring Christians of different communions closer together, because the new understanding of the Liturgy is overcoming various distorting prejudices and defective ideas which all the communions of the west have inherited from the Middle Ages and which explain, in part, their divisions. In the Roman Church [and this is, of course, true of other Churches too] the movement has been strongly pastoral in character, and it is the strongest force now working for the renewal of the Christian life among ordinary people.[1]

There is a general acceptance, for example, of the fact that the eucharist is the central act of worship in the Church and that it is a corporate action in which all must share. On the one hand the Free Churches are prepared to admit that it is wrong to regard the eucharist as an infrequent 'extra'

[1] Charles Davis, 'Church Architecture and Liturgy' in *Towards a Church Architecture*, edited P. Hammond (1962), p. 112.

service. *Orders and Prayers for Church Worship*, produced by Dr. E. A. Payne and Stephen Winward in 1960 primarily for Baptist ministers, states quite categorically in its Introduction, 'It is a departure from apostolic worship to celebrate the Lord's Supper infrequently, or to regard it as an appendage following another service.'[1] On the Roman Catholic side there is the recognition that non-communicating attendance at the eucharist—even if frequent—is inadequate. The Vatican Council's *Constitution on the Sacred Liturgy* declares that the faithful should not be present at Mass 'as strangers or silent spectators . . . they should be instructed by God's Word, and be nourished at the table of the Lord's Body'.[2] It is interesting to note too that this statement refers to the Word as well as the Sacrament. The Gospel is proclaimed by both, and neither must be neglected. This readiness to see the eucharist in its true perspective has been accompanied by a growing agreement on eucharistic doctrine—that it is Christ who is the true celebrant, that the Great Prayer is one of thanksgiving over bread and wine for all the mighty acts of God in creation and redemption, that there is no re-immolation of Christ, and that his is the one all-sufficient sacrifice in which we all, as members of his body, share.

At the same time the liturgy must have a 'shape' or well-defined pattern. This does not deny for one moment the value of free prayer, an element in public worship which some Churches value highly. But free prayer should grow out of the set prayer of the Church. Worship should find room for both, and it would be wrong to set one against the other. *Orders and Prayers for Church Worship* expresses it admirably: 'We must avoid on the one hand the dangers taught us by history of an inflexible and fixed liturgy which

[1] E. A. Payne and S. S. F. Winward, *Orders and Prayers for Church Worship* (1960), p. xii.
[2] *Constitution on the Sacred Liturgy*, chap. 2, sc. 48.

leaves no room for the freedom of the Holy Spirit. On the other hand, we must avoid that "squalid sluttery" and un-inspired disorder which comes from disregarding the tradi-tional pattern and forms of Christian worship.'[1] There is nothing to fear in the idea of a liturgy. Liturgy is not to be identified with a rigid form and mechanical repetition. Liturgy emphasizes the corporateness of worship: and the intelligent and effective offering of worship demands services with a shape and recognizable forms of words.

There is, too, an increasing perception of the importance of Initiation. Whether it be infant baptism or believer's baptism, few would deny that the rite involves identification with our Lord's baptism, involving a participation in his life and membership of his body. The baptized Christian lives for Christ's sake and for the sake of the world: the sacred and the secular are inextricably bound together. Life 'in Christ' manifests itself in a variety of ways—in membership of such communities as those of Iona or Taizé, in groups of worker-priests or industrial missions, in the house-church or the district meeting or the cell. But no matter how the Christian life is manifested, entry into it not only confers divine gifts and a privileged status, but also demands responsibilities. Baptism is therefore no private and indiscriminate action, but one to be administered publicly and after careful considera-tion and preparation on the part of adult baptizands or parents and godparents in the case of infants.

Or consider the observance of the Christian Year. Once disregarded by many Churches of the Reformation, its value is once again coming to be appreciated. The experience of the Church of Scotland is typical. Thirty years ago it pro-duced *Prayers for the Christian Year*, accepting the desirability of observing 'those great occasions when the transcendent

---

[1] Payne and Winward, op. cit., pp. xiv-xv.

facts of the Christian Faith are the subjects of commemoration. . . . Further, the Church of Scotland believes in the fellowship of all believers, as implied in the doctrine of the Holy Catholic Church and the Communion of Saints. The commemorations . . . afford it inspiring opportunities of bearing witness to that element in its faith, by uniting *ex animo* with the Holy Church throughout all the world, in celebrating the fundamental certainties which are held in common by all believers.'[1] Since then the observance of the Church's Year has made great progress in Scotland, and in 1952 a new edition of the book was produced with additional commemorations. The Church's Year reveals the whole mystery of the saving events of our Lord's life: and fundamental to the commemoration of those saving events is the weekly celebration of Sunday. Every Sunday, the Lord's Day, is a little Easter: it is the eighth day, the day of his Resurrection. The early Christians recognized the Lord's Supper as a feast of the Resurrection and a foretaste of the Heavenly Banquet, to which they looked forward in their prayer, *Maranatha*, 'Come, Lord Jesus'. By their proper celebration of Sunday, Christians of today also have the same vision, identify themselves with their Lord and his work, and affirm their citizenship of Heaven.

Again, a word must be said about church architecture; for the growing agreement on ideas about worship is being reflected in the design and arrangement of the buildings in which worship takes place. The building must serve the liturgy. The emphasis on the eucharist, the awareness of the significance of baptism, the importance of the ministry of the word, the need for congregational participation, the extension of worship into mission—these are all factors which influence the siting of a church, its size, its shape and its

[1] *Prayers for the Christian Year*, preface to the 1st edition, 1935.

furnishing. Already they have produced a revolution in Church design which has broken down denominational barriers, particularly on the Continent. In churches which have been built or redesigned to meet the needs of the Liturgical Movement, it is no longer easy to decide the denomination to which they belong. One of the most re-markable examples of this in Great Britain is the restored Roman Catholic cathedral in Aberdeen: it is said that some visitors have found it difficult to believe that it does not owe its allegiance to Geneva rather than to Rome!

The same phenomenon is apparent in the realm of hymnody, and here I cannot do better than quote the com-ment of an expert, Dr. Erik Routley, when the *Baptist Hymn Book* and the *English Hymnal Service Book* appeared within a fortnight of each other in 1962.

In, let us say, the year 1920, if you picked up a hymn book, you could tell in a couple of minutes by examining its contents whether it came from the Church of England or Dissent. If it were Anglican-high, it would attend carefully to the Church's Year and draw largely on the writings of the Victorian bishops. If it were Anglican-evangelical, it would be a very fat book con-taining large additions from the Victorian gentlewomen and the post-Sankey revivalists. If it were of Dissent or Methodism, it would contain much of Watts (and/or Wesley), and be theologi-cally arranged, but probably it would disregard the Ascension. Musically you would always see evidences of a certain disdain for history and a corresponding enthusiasm for popular pleasure of the pious kind in the Dissenting books, while the Anglican ones would display the qualities of reaction from the climate of Trollope. In our time, the only way you can distinguish between an Anglican and a Dissenting book in plain covers is to check whether it contains 'Eternal Light' by Thomas Binney. If it doesn't, it's Anglican. This is enormously important. Whatever happens here is at once noticed there.[1]

[1] Erik Routley, 'Praises Renewed and Reformed' in *The British Weekly*, 15 March 1962.

Finally, there is the growing realization that the mission of the Church is inextricably bound up with its worship. There is no dichotomy between faith and works, nor between the Church's godward and manward activities. The Body of Christ is a priestly people, itself redeemed by God and entrusted by him with the task of proclaiming his triumphs.[1] This fact is quite crucial; and its importance has been emphasized in this book by making it the subject of the concluding, and longest, essay. Many other of the points referred to here are also discussed in greater detail in the following pages. But sufficient has been said, I hope, to justify this experiment in liturgical co-operation. It would be rash to expect miracles: and one thing we do not envisage is a dull uniformity in the ways of worship in this country as a whole. We can hope, however, to make some modest contribution to the cause of Christian unity and help the Church fulfil its true function in the world today. The prospects before us are admirably expressed by Dr. Howard G. Hageman, a distinguished scholar of the Dutch Reformed Church in America:

The Liturgical Movement is a new frontier on which all Churches, regardless of the rigidity of their liturgical traditions, now find themselves. In the common exploration of what is for all of us, in one way or another, new material, we are bound to reach easier ecumenical conversation. I do not know where these new agreements may take us; I should be suspicious of any attempt to over-play their importance. But the fact remains that the Liturgy is the most fruitful area for ecumenical exploration. If that fact is recognized and, in the best sense of the word, exploited, we shall know what the next step may be.[2]

[1] Pet. ii. 9–10.
[2] H. G. Hageman, 'The Coming-of-Age of the Liturgical Movement' in *Studia Liturgica*, vol. ii, no. 4 (December 1963), p. 263.

THE CHURCH AT WORSHIP

R. D. WHITEHORN

To speak of the Church at worship implies that Christians are in community with one another. However ancient or modern may be the divisions between Christians, however widely they may diverge in their interpretation of doctrine or practice in worship, all have in common the belief that man must have a right relationship to God, he must be 'in Christ'. That is what distinguishes Christians from non-Christians; and this is what makes the Christian community. This community may be a highly centralized hierarchy or a much looser company of believers; but in every case the community contains and comprises all the 'ministry' and all the 'laity'—every member of the community has 'access by the one Spirit to the Father'; every member ought to be a worshipper; and the worship of the community ought to unite the members, whatever their part in the worship, as 'one body in Christ Jesus'.

Worship is 'worth-ship' or shaping the worth of God. It is 'giving God the glory due to his Name'.[1] It is the response of the creature to the Creator. 'Anyone who comes to God must believe that he exists and that he rewards those who search for him.'[2] The Church at worship is a community of Christians to each of whom in some way and in some degree God has shown himself. 'Canst thou by searching find out God?'

[1] *Senior Catechism of the Methodist Church*, 47. [2] Heb. xi. 6, N.E.B.

No. But God reveals himself in his creative power, in his holiness, his justice and his mercy. Man's response is indicated by the way in which he lives and uses God's gifts. Not only his prayers but also his work, his recreation and his relations with his fellows are all worship, in so far as they shape or reflect the worth of God.

There is one word in the Christian vocabulary which perhaps illustrates the meaning of worship better than any other—the word 'liturgy'. Liturgy is derived from the two small Greek words *laos*, which means people, and *ergon*, which means work. They therefore suggest work or service of a public kind. In ancient Greece 'liturgy' denoted a service rendered to the state. A citizen might be required to equip, man and sail a warship for a given period; or he might be required to finance a group to be sent on some religious errand; or he might be required to provide a chorus for some great festival. In each case the service he rendered was his 'liturgy'. Later the Greek translators of the Old Testament used the word in the Septuagint to translate the Hebrew word *sharath*, which meant to minister on behalf of the community, and with particular reference to the worship of the Temple.[1] From the Old Testament there was a natural transition to its use in the New Testament. Zacharias therefore exercised his 'liturgy' in the Temple according to the custom of his priestly office,[2] while the Epistle to the Hebrews speaks of priests daily 'liturgizing' and offering sacrifices.[3] Nevertheless the New Testament does not confine its use simply to the religious functions of particular people. St. Paul uses it to describe service in a wider context. Magistrates, in the performance of their duties, are liturgists or ministers of God;[4] while elsewhere he uses

---

[1] e.g. Num. viii. 22, 25; xviii. 4; 2 Chron. viii. 14.   [2] Luke i. 8–9.
[3] Heb. x. 11.   [4] Rom. xiii. 6.

it in its original sense of acts of service or charity to others.[1]

Now from these various uses certain points emerge which give meaning to its subsequent use in the worship of the Church. In the Greek Septuagint it was commonly used with the word *ecclesia*, the translation of the Hebrew word *qahal*, which referred to the sacred assembly of all Israel—the people of God—assembled for worship.[2] It was the whole people who 'liturgized'. Liturgy was a corporate action; and this was what St. Peter was referring to when he described the Christian community as 'an elect race, a royal priesthood, a holy nation'.[3] Liturgy therefore described the individual's contribution to a corporate act of worship. St. Clement of Rome, writing to the Christians of Corinth about A.D. 95, urged each of the brethren, in his own order, to give thanks to God, 'adhering to the appointed rule of his liturgy with all reverence'.[4] On the other hand, the word also described the duties of the sacred ministry as distinct from the rest of the people—'clergy' as distinct from 'laity'. St. Ignatius, writing a little later (A.D. 110–17), pointed out that what distinguished the liturgical *ecclesia* from an ordinary gathering of people was the fact that the ministry was present to exercise their liturgical functions—'without these it is not called an *ecclesia*'.[5]

On any doctrine of the ministry, it was acceptable and necessary that Christian worship should be led by those whom the community chose as best fitted for it, and appropriate that these should be set apart or ordained to exercise their liturgy with and for the community. Whatever other duties and responsibilities they exercised, the liturgy was and is the great corporate action of the Church. The ministry *to* the Church, in Word and Sacrament, is a gift of Christ by

---

[1] 2 Cor. ix. 12; Phil. ii. 17, 25, 30.   [2] e.g. Ps. lxxxv. 5–6.   [3] 1 Pet. ii. 9.
[4] 1 Clement xli.   [5] Trallians iii. 1; cf. Philadelphians iv; Smyrnaeans viii.

the Holy Spirit to foster and maintain the ministry *of* the whole Church, the 'royal priesthood', the 'people claimed by God for his own'.[1]

A further point to be remembered is that when the Old Testament spoke of the assembly or people of God, it was speaking of a community which was conscious of their unique covenant relationship with God. All the members of this community had a common heritage and a common destiny. In the New Testament this was equally true of the Church, the new Israel. They are the Body of Christ, of which he himself is the head. They are the people whom he has chosen not only to receive the work of salvation but also to witness to it in the world. They are a chosen people with a service or liturgy to God and also a service or liturgy to men. They are a Church with a mission—to work for the extension of the rule of God, in the moral, social and political life of the world: and in worship the Church as a body recognizes its earthly meaning and purpose. Jesus Christ is continually carrying out the great work of salvation he received from the Father through the Church. When the Word of God is proclaimed and the sacraments are ministered, Jesus Christ is present.

Now if such principles of Christian worship have been generally accepted by the Christian community, it is nevertheless obvious that there has been diversity in practice, in the *form* rather than in the *content* expressing the response of man to God's grace and gift. On this point some sentences of the late Dr. A. E. Garvie, the Congregational theologian, may be quoted.

Although all my own inclinations and tastes are to desire an approach to God with 'the thinnest human veil between' (Browning), yet I am compelled to ask myself whether this in-

[1] I Pet. ii. 9, N.E.B.

difference to form is altogether justified. God has in wisdom, power, and goodness woven as the garment in which we see His presence and activity a material Universe with all its variety, beauty, abundance, and vastness. . . . Man has aesthetic sense to appreciate and aesthetic talent to reproduce beauty of shape, colour, and sound. May not beauty claim a place in religion with truth and goodness? It is in worship that it can most fully be expressed. . . . May not our worship have lost its attractiveness for many because it does not satisfy the whole man with all his varied interests? If there is ever to be a closer union of the Christian Churches this question will need to be candidly and seriously considered; but meanwhile let those who dislike any ritual and those who feel their need of it learn to love one another in Christ; and here as elsewhere love will find the way to mutual understanding and appreciation of differences in the approach to the one Father, revealed in the One Saviour and Lord and experienced through the one Holy Spirit.[1]

The important thing is that the worshipping company of Christians in church (or indeed a solitary worshipper in his home) should be able to receive the Word of the grace of God and respond to it. The form of worship in the Church has never been exactly the same. Even when the words of worship have had uniformity in a large part of the Christian community, there has been diversity within it in the external acts and accompaniments. The sung eucharist in a small Anglican church could hardly pretend to the same beauty of music, or splendour of vestments, or symbolism of movement, as a great cathedral can provide. The service and preaching of the Word in a village chapel might be simpler than a city congregation would hear to its profit. Yet in all four God's grace is offered, Christ is present, and man makes his response. It is no disparagement of any of them to believe that in none of them is the *form* of the worship of ultimate

[1] A. E. Garvie, 'The Philosophy of Worship' in *Christian Worship*, edited by N. Micklem (1936), pp. 17–18.

importance. There is danger of spiritual pride in attaching profound doctrinal significance to all the details of our forms of worship. There is room for variety. 'There are varieties of gifts, but the same Spirit. There are varieties of service, but the same Lord. There are many forms of work, but all of them, in all men, are the work of the same God.'[1]

It is also interesting to note that a uniformity in the words of worship has not produced a uniformity in belief. Certain words used in worship have acquired different shades of meaning; and it is over these shades of meaning that most of the differences have arisen among Christians of the various traditions. The use of the term 'sacrifice' in the eucharist is a typical example. Nevertheless, despite such differences, it should not be forgotten that Christians are at one in their faith in the effectual gift in the eucharist of God's grace in Christ through the Holy Spirit and in the response of their worshipful thanksgiving. In this connexion some words of the Archbishop of Canterbury are very relevant.

It is as possible to speak of 'the Liturgy' underlying its many presentations as it is to speak of 'the Gospel' underlying the four Gospels. All have certain common elements. In all there is *thanksgiving*; in all there is *commemoration*; in all there is the note of *mystery* since Christ is present to feed His people; in all there is the *fellowship* of those who are united with one another and with the whole Church, and in all Christ gives Himself in *sacrifice*. . . . *Mystery* means that . . . the presence of His body and His blood is not the result of the individual's faith, but, like the Incarnation itself, a presence of Jesus which faith may receive and which un-faith may reject. . . . Of the *mystery* there were, in the Church of the first five centuries, several explanations all held within the Church's tolerant embrace. Thus some patristic writers simply assert that Christ feeds the souls of men, without explaining how; some use language of 'type' and 'symbol' and 'representation';

[1] 1 Cor. xii. 4–6, N.E.B.

some emphasize a change wrought in the elements by consecration so that they are the body and blood of Jesus while still remaining also bread and wine. The Church was content that these theories should be held side by side.[1]

We should be wise to do the same.

Finally we should remember that the corporate life and common worship of the Christian community both vitalizes and depends upon the spiritual life of its members. Public worship ought to enhance in every worshipper the sense of the grace of God, to be experienced in his own personal religious life and devotion. His own private prayers, of thanksgiving, penitence, assurance and intercession, ought to be a preparation for and a continuance of the prayers of the community; and therefore the form and language of public worship should enable him to bear his part in it. It is not something *done for him* by priest or minister, but something which *he is doing*, he and his fellow worshippers together; something which each of them, when they separate, will seek to continue individually as members of the Body of Christ. 'The public worship will be formal unless the private devotion is fervent. . . . The one cannot be a substitute for the other, and must seek its complement therein.'[2]

There are many ways in which individuals have related their private devotion to public worship. Family worship is one way; Bible reading with the various aids to its understanding is another. The observance of the Christian Year and of Saints' Days, the use of books of Hours or of collections of prayers and the like—all can be used in the remembrance that fellow Christians are in similar ways trying to observe some discipline of worship: and set times during the day may best help continuance and regularity. Whatever

[1] A. M. Ramsey, *The Gospel and the Catholic Church* (1936), pp. 110–12.
[2] A. E. Garvie, op. cit., pp. 9–11.

means be used, our fellowship in Christ with the whole Christian community should be present to our hearts and minds, sharing with the Church at worship 'the unity of the Spirit in the bond of peace'. It would be well to take to heart some words of the Dean of St. Paul's, Dr. W. R. Matthews:

There is much to be said on the need for agreement in belief before we can join in worship. . . . But there is also much to be said in favour of starting with worship. For one thing, we can begin now to meet together for prayer and praise: we can attend each other's churches and feel the warmth of each other's faith and love without waiting to criticize the theology. The truth is, of course, that doctrine and worship go together and when separated languish. Doctrine without worship is only an exercise in metaphysics, while worship without doctrine declines into 'uplift': but if we really want to begin creating unity without delay we had better start with worship.[1]

[1] In the *Daily Telegraph*, 18 January 1964.

LITURGY AND UNITY[1]

J. A. LAMB

THERE is wide agreement to the proposition that its unity is one of the most urgent of the problems facing the Church. Some indeed suggest that other matters such as the missionary task or the battle with secularism and communism are more important; but in fact many who are engaged on these great works discover that the divided thrust of the Church is a real source of weakness. Some feel that disunity does not really create a problem except to a few enthusiasts and are ready to claim, 'We are doing very well as we are.' Some feel little if any sense of shame at our 'unhappy divisions'; they suggest that the present situation is due to historical causes and that it is an inheritance which we have to accept. Some would lay the emphasis on the spiritual unity which they claim is all that is required. Their argument seems to be: 'Let us agree that we are all one in Christ; let us work together on moral and social problems; but there is no need to come together for the central and essential duty of the Church, in the worship of God.' This argument must seem very strange to the outsider and does indeed seem very horrid to many within the Church. For whatever reason we may turn away from this problem, we are brought back to it again and again, sometimes by the logic of the situation,

[1] The substance of this essay was published in the *Church Service Society Annual* for 1960 and appears here in a revised form with the consent of the Society.

sometimes by the pressure of necessity, sometimes by a great longing in the heart for a closer, deeper, more vital fellowship. Admittedly there are great difficulties in the way, as the discussions of recent times have made clear, though it is important to remember that many of these discussions could not have taken place at all sixty years ago.

We are to investigate the relation between liturgy and unity; and liturgy we take here in its wider sense, as the worship of the Church. Does the worship of the Church in any way suggest or express its unity? Can liturgy help towards unity? Let us begin with a glance at the scriptural attitude.

It is difficult to believe that our Lord ever thought of the Church except as one. His high-priestly prayer, 'that they all may be one', makes that clear. The book of Acts pictures the essential unity of the Church. The early Christians felt themselves to be one. They had all things common; they adhered to the apostles' doctrine and fellowship, breaking bread from house to house; they supported one another in time of need, and the multiplication of local congregations throughout the Empire made no cleavage of the unity. St. Paul gives us a fuller exposition. He has no sympathy with any division in the Church. 'Now I beseech you, brethren, by the name of our Lord Jesus Christ, that ye all speak the same thing, and that there be no schisms among you; but that ye be perfectly joined together in the same mind and in the same judgment.'[1]

What is the ground for this view? There is one God, one Lord, one Spirit. 'There are diversities of gifts, but the same Spirit. And there are differences of administrations, but the same Lord; and there are diversities of operations, but it is the same God who worketh all in all.'[2] He goes on to expound

[1] I Cor. i. 10; cf. Rom. xv. 5–6; Eph. iv. 1–3; Phil. ii. 2.
[2] I Cor. xii. 4–6; cf. Eph. iv. 3–6.

the working and influences of the Holy Spirit, and urges that, though there are many members, there is but one body. Since God is one, his call is one, and the communication of life in Christ is one. In fact the Christian experience carries us on to the affirmation of the unity of the Church, because the Christian experience brings us into the Body of Christ, which is one. For St. Paul 'there is one faith', consisting of certain fundamental subjects essential to the being of every Christian, essential to the being of the Church. The basis of this faith was expressed in the earliest form of the confession, 'Jesus is Lord', which is perhaps not so simple as it seems, implying not only a profession of faith in him as Master, but also a suggestion of the messianic sense of the word 'Lord'; and further, a suggestion that he is Lord of all, if not in actuality, certainly in an eschatological sense.

Two symbols of unity which belong to the Body are the sacraments of baptism and the Lord's supper. By baptism we become members of the Body, and this ordinance which unites all Christians to the one Christ and in his one death and resurrection, manifests as well as establishes the unity. 'By one Spirit are we all baptized into one body';[1] and again, 'As many of you as have been baptized into Christ have put on Christ . . . ye are all one in Christ Jesus'.[2] The other sacrament is also a sign of unity. 'We being many are one bread and one body; for we are all partakers of that one bread',[3] or as the Revised Standard Version puts it, 'Because there is one loaf, we who are many are one body, for we all partake of the same loaf.' The fact that the bread is the communion of the Body of Christ emphasizes the eucharist as a symbol of unity.

There can be no doubt that the New Testament thinks of the Church as one and undivided, and that in more than a spiritual sense. To say that the unity belongs to the invisible

---

[1] I Cor. xii. 13.   [2] Gal. iii. 27.   [3] I Cor. x. 17.

Church only, as some allege, would suggest that it is possible
to be united in the invisible Church but divided in the historic
Churches. Surely there is something wrong if we can believe
that in the Church triumphant we may find ourselves at the
messianic table beside those whom we cannot join at the
eucharistic table. The Scriptures intend to speak of and
portray an organic unity in the Church.

The Fathers of the Church witness to the same truth.
There was the same insistence on unity as a note of the
Church, and the same tests and symbols were used. The
Faith was still a test of unity. The Creed was the canon, the
regula fidei, the standard by which orthodoxy and heresy
were distinguished. One of the Fathers said, 'There is one
rule of faith alone which is entirely unchangeable, irreform-
able, namely, to believe in one God Almighty, Founder of
the world, and in his Son Jesus Christ, born of the Virgin
Mary. . . .'[1] This is a view to which most of the Fathers would
subscribe. In particular we must note the views on questions
of worship. There was for long no insistence on uniformity
in worship, in rites or in ceremonies, as a sign of unity. The
historian Eusebius recorded Irenaeus as saying, 'We all keep
peace with one another, and the divergence of our ways
of fasting only commends our agreement in the faith.'[2]
Similarly St. Augustine stated, 'In those things about which
there is no prescription in the divine scriptures, the customs
of God's people or the institution of our forefathers are to be
regarded as laws. For if we dispute about such matters and
condemn the custom of one church by that of another, there
will arise interminable contention.'[3] It may be added that the
two Sacraments were everywhere regarded as essential to the
life of the Church and as symbols of its unity.

---

[1] Tertullian, *De virgin. veland.* i.   [2] Eusebius, *Ecclesiastical History*, V. 24.
[3] Augustine, *Ep. 86, Ad Casulanum.*

If we look at the period of the Reformation, which has often seemed so disastrous to the unity of the Church, it is important to remember that schism was not at all the intention of the reformers, who sought a radical reformation of the Church from within. Even when we reflect on the political and social influences which added their weight to the demand for reform, the fact remains that the movement was chiefly religious in its inspiration. It is curious, no doubt, that all this seething demand should run into separate and different channels which became more and more stereotyped, and more and more emphasized the differences; so much so that today the tremendous task before us is to direct these channels nearer to each other and ultimately into one great stream whose strength will suffice to sweep away all that keeps the Church from the success of its mission. But the important thing is that the leading reformers all abhorred the idea of schism and adhered to the doctrine of the unity of the Church. They continued, for example, to use the Apostles' Creed as an expression of the Faith, though it was expanded into confessions of varying length and detail. Thus Calvin in his Catechism said that the creed is 'the formula of confession which all Christians have in common';[1] and again, he urged that where the Word was purely preached and reverently heard, and the Sacraments were administered according to the institution of Christ, men were to recognize the Church and not to contend against it or separate themselves from it. To depart from the Church was to deny God and Christ. All the reformers would agree on that position.

Space forbids us to go into detail about the many movements towards closer fellowship between the Churches, or the various attempts towards accommodation which have taken place since the Reformation. Nor can we spend time on the

[1] *Institutes*, IV. i. 10.

splits and secessions which have disrupted the Church in the same period, only giving thanks that many of them have already been healed. But it is clear that the Church has never been satisfied with less than true unity, has never recognized a state of schism as Christian, and has never forgotten the deep meaning or the serious challenge of our Lord's words—*that they all may be one.*

We turn now to the examination of the relation between liturgy and unity. It seems that this relation has been somewhat neglected and that it should be studied more widely and more deeply. Its importance lies in this, that worship is the chief function of the Church. The Church has other functions such as evangelism and ministry. Some would regard mission, for example, as equal to worship in importance. Nevertheless, it would be widely agreed that the worship of God is the source of power and of inspiration for all other functions. Moreover, while the Church Militant has various functions here on earth, the only function remaining in the Church Triumphant will, it seems, be worship. That is why this relationship between worship and unity seems so important. Now the various traditions of worship are from many points of view very different, and the emphasis within each part of the Church is laid upon the tradition within that part. But perhaps the differences should receive less emphasis, and the elements in worship common to all should be underlined. It is time to seek for the harmony of the patterns.

Let us look first of all at some of the distinctive characteristics in the service books of some of the different Churches. In the Roman books we have the use of Latin, which seems to impart a certain indefinable tone not to be found elsewhere. The rites are almost entirely priestly and the share of the people has traditionally been very small, though the Liturgical Movement is making a great difference. The service which all Catholics have a duty to attend is the Mass, though some extra-liturgical services such as Benediction are popular. Secondly, the Anglican Communion is wedded to some form of the *Book of Common Prayer*, which is meant to be in the hands of every worshipper; and the form of the services in which people can so largely share expresses perhaps better than elsewhere the corporate nature of worship. The *Book of Common Prayer* contains two kinds of service in addition to the Occasional Offices, namely, the Daily Offices and the Holy Communion. The services are wholly prescribed, though there is much difference from parish to parish in the way the services are performed. Thirdly, in most other Churches the services are not prescribed, the forms used being decided on by the individual minister or the congregation. Service books are provided for the guidance of leaders of worship, but there is no compulsion to follow them. Nevertheless, the influence of such books as the Scottish *Book of Common Order 1940*, the Methodist *Book of Offices*, the Congregational *A Book of Public Worship* and *A Book of Services and Prayers*, and the Baptist *Orders and Prayers for Church Worship* has been strong, with the result that there is perhaps rather less variety than in the past: but this freedom and variety signify something of value, the loss of which would undoubtedly be grievous. In this group also there are two types of service, the ordinary preaching service and the Lord's Supper. One feature here is the small part taken by the people. In many places, apart from the items of praise in psalm and hymn, the people are silent.

We have, therefore, three types of service which appear to have not only different traditions behind them, but also real differences in idea and in practice, and it looks as if any kind of collaboration would be difficult to achieve. But in spite of this, there is much that is common to all; and these common elements we must now investigate.

First of all, the *subjects* in the forms of worship are the same. All the services are founded on Holy Scripture, readings from which are of fundamental importance, for everywhere the proclamation of the Word of God must be regarded as of first concern.

The principle by which the readings are chosen varies; in one case a prescribed lectionary may be used, while in another the lections are chosen freely by the minister. But that matters little. The important thing is that the Scriptures are read and the Gospel proclaimed.

The subjects of prayer are the same—adoration, confession, supplication, thanksgiving and intercession. The shape of the prayers may differ, some sections of the Church preferring the brief collect form which is easily followed by the hearer, and others preferring the longer, more discursive prayer which makes heavy demands on the attention. But wherever men turn to God, the great themes already mentioned are found. In particular, there are few places nowadays where the Lord's Prayer is not used in worship. The prayer which Christ gave to his disciples at their request must always fill an important place in the approach of God's children to their Heavenly Father.

The materials used for praise in the services are also a common possession of the whole Church. The use of the Psalter is obvious in this respect; for every section of the Church in every century of the Christian era has used this book with appreciation and joy. There is no kind of service, however simple or elaborate, that has altogether rejected the Psalms. It is true that there have been times and places when the Psalter has suffered neglect. The Roman services for example, both the Daily Offices and the Mass, in the process of time greatly reduced the amount of psalmody: but recently the desire has been expressed to put psalmody on a firmer foundation and to give it a larger place in worship. The Second Vatican Council[1] has determined that the Psalms are to be recited no longer weekly 'but through some longer period of time', in order that the Offices may be better arranged. The same desire to make a better use of the Psalter has been seen elsewhere, as in the revision of the prose Psalms carried out by the Church of England,[2] or in the revision of the metrical psalter in the Presbyterian Church of Ireland some years ago, or in the demand for revision elsewhere.

One of the most successful pieces of work on the Psalms has been the rhythmic translation by Joseph Gelineau, which has achieved wide popularity in France, and which in its recent English version has been warmly welcomed. The most significant fact here is that the Gelineau psalmody, though Roman Catholic in origin, has been so acceptable and successful in many Protestant circles, a tribute to the ecumenical value of the Psalms.

If we consider the question of hymnody it is evident that though a hymn book may be issued by a particular denomination the contents are never confined to compositions written by members of that denomination. Every hymn book is ecumenical in its choice of material, and many hymns appear in books of a very different nature. Thus the *Revised Church Hymnary* does not exclude plainsong music or hymns from medieval and Roman Catholic sources; while the *English Hymnal* includes hymns by Calvinistic evangelical writers like Isaac Watts and John Newton. The same catholicity applies to *Hymns Ancient and Modern, Congregational Praise,*

---

[1] *Constitution on the Sacred Liturgy* (1963), sc. 91.
[2] *The Revised Psalter.* The Final text as approved by the Convocations of Canterbury and York, October 1963 (London, S.P.C.K.).

the *Methodist Hymn Book* and the new *Baptist Hymn Book*. There is a universal claim that Christian hymnody belongs not to any one group but to all: and indeed at the present time there is a widening body of opinion in favour of the preparation of a hymn book by a joint committee representing many denominations of varied traditions for use by all. A hymn book also contains music as well as words, and it is clear from the examination of any hymnary that the choice of music is as wide as that of the words. Indeed, it might be said that the Liturgical Movement is broadening the attitude to church music in a quite general way, just as the broadcast and television religious services reveal the values in the worship of different denominations.

Another item which has long been used in worship is the Creed. In many churches the Apostles' Creed is recited as a statement of proclamation of the Church's belief, and in the Communion service the Nicene Creed similarly finds a place. These forms provide the worshipper, and indeed also the outsider, with a summary of the faith. Admittedly there are reservations in some Churches about the use of the Creed, and even where it is regularly recited there are very varied interpretations of its clauses. Nevertheless, Principal W. A. Curtis's statement that the Apostles' Creed 'to the common mind of Christendom stands as next to Holy Writ the most venerable bond of unity and the symbol of harmonious faith',[1] is largely true. Finally the two sacraments of baptism and the Lord's supper must be noticed, both of which are regarded as of dominical institution and therefore as essential to the life of the Church.

In the second place, there is much that is common in the *form* or *structure* of the services. This might seem to be an obvious deduction from the fact that all the Churches claim

[1] W. A. Curtis, *History of Creeds and Confessions of Faith* (1911), p. 63.

the New Testament as the source and authority of their worship. Some would argue for the right to develop the forms and to add this or that to the original, while others would set limitations to this right, or even perhaps deny any right of development. The process of time has thus brought about many differences in the content of the services, not only by additions but in some cases by changing the order within the services. Any examination of the service books of the Churches will make this obvious. But first appearances may prove to be deceptive when the orders of service are examined more closely. There are three types of service which we may consider briefly. First there are what we may call the ordinary morning and evening services which correspond to Matins and Evensong in the *Book of Common Prayer*. As we have seen, all these contain psalmody and hymnody, prayers and Scripture lessons; and although Matins and Evensong do not mention the sermon (which really belongs to the service of Holy Communion), this is frequently preached at these Offices. Hence it is often assumed that there is some relationship between the normal morning service of the Free Churches and Anglican Matins. This is certainly true of the Methodist *Book of Offices*, in which Morning Prayer is practically the service of Anglican Matins. But elsewhere the relationship if any is slight, though the *Book of Common Prayer* has exerted a strong influence in some quarters. In fact, as Professor W. D. Maxwell has shown,[1] the ordinary morning preaching service of the Reformed Churches (that is, those derived from the Calvinist tradition) is a truncated Communion service, and some bodies not so closely related to Calvin are accepting this position for themselves.[2] The

---

[1] See W. D. Maxwell, *John Knox's Genevan Service Book, 1556* (Edinburgh, 1931).

[2] Cf. *Orders and Prayers for Church Worship* (Baptist, 1960), p. xii; *A Book of Public Worship* (Congregationalist, 1948), pp. xi ff.

view is that the fullness of worship will be attained only when the Word and the Sacrament are brought together as they were at the first.[1] The medieval Church separated these two essentials in worship, but the desire of most of the Reformers was to return to the primitive wholeness of worship. Zwingli appears to have been the only Reformer to differ from this position, since he separated Word and Sacrament, and it has been suggested that he had a strong influence on the English Puritans,[2] so that in some cases preaching services did not have the close connexion with the Communion service which held good elsewhere. But in spite of that, these services are built on much the same pattern.

This is more profoundly true of Holy Communion. Every form of this service is derived from the fourfold action of our Lord at the Institution of the Supper—he took; he blessed; he brake; he gave. Round these basic actions have grown up many accompaniments, some of which are found almost universally, and others less nearly so. Thus we find the Words of Institution read as a warrant or contained in the Eucharistic Prayer, the Consecration Prayer itself including thanks to God for creation and for redemption, a special acknowledgement of the gift of Christ and all he did for us, and in many cases the Epiclesis, or prayer that the Holy Spirit should come to bless the elements and sometimes also those who partake of them.[3] Always there must appear the Fraction or Breaking of Bread, the Communion and the Post-Communion Prayer. Certain formulas, such as the *Sursum Corda* and the *Sanctus*, have also appeared for centuries. The position of these elements varies from church to

---

[1] Cf. Oscar Cullmann, *Early Christian Worship* (1953), pp. 26 ff.

[2] Cf. R. L. Bainton, *The Reformation of the Sixteenth Century* (1953), p. 86.

[3] The Epiclesis is present in the Book of Common Prayer of 1549, the Scottish Liturgy of 1657 and that of 1929, the *Book of Common Order 1940*, the Congregationalist and Baptist books, but not in the Roman Missal, Book of Common Prayer 1662, or the Methodist *Book of Offices*.

church, and in revision discussions at the present time the
order is a subject of considerable importance.

It follows from this that there is much in common in the
Order of Holy Communion in the various service books,
and it is of special interest that the Church of South India,
which is a union of Anglicans, Methodists, Presbyterians and
Congregationalists, has been able to agree on a eucharistic
rite which appears in their *Book of Common Worship* (1963),
and which is recognisably related to the Orders of the
separate Churches. If this can be achieved in India, there is
surely hope that the Churches in our own land may be able
to produce an Order acceptable to all.

The same is true of the baptismal service. The salient
features appear almost everywhere—the prayer for the blessing of the water,[1] the brief address with the scriptural warrant,
the profession of faith, including in some cases the renuncia-
tions, the administration of the sacrament by pouring on or
sprinkling with or immersing in water, the baptismal formula, and a post-baptismal prayer.

It seems therefore that in the structure of the services in the
various books many similarities are revealed; and this should
be a factor tending towards deeper mutual understanding.
It must be recognized, however, that in spite of similarities in
form, there are deep divergences in doctrine. There is still
much argument about the theological significance of baptism,
of confirmation, of the eucharist and particularly of the
eucharistic sacrifice. Nevertheless it seems very important
that here again the common features should receive greater
emphasis, in order to strengthen the desire for closer fellowship in worship.

Finally one may suggest that in the services the *intention* is

[1] In the Roman Missal, the Book of Common Prayer, the Scottish Liturgy, and
the *Book of Common Order 1940*, though not in the Methodist, Congregational, or
Baptist books.

the same. The Council of Trent taught that for the valid con-
ferring of the sacraments the minister must have the intention of doing at least what the Church does; while today
there is required a real internal intention to act as a minister
of Christ, or to do what Christ instituted the sacraments to
effect.[1] It may be said that in the various forms of service in
other Churches the intention is always the same, namely, to
do what Christ commanded us to do, to proclaim his Gospel,
to evangelize the world for him, to teach whatsoever he
taught, to baptize in the Name of the Trinity, to celebrate
the Holy Supper, which he 'did institute and in his holy
gospel command us to continue, a perpetual memorial of
that his precious death and sacrifice until his coming again'.[2]
The intention is simply to obey the Lord and Master. There
may be different interpretations of what obedience requires,
and different methods of obedience; but it seems to be of
some importance that the intention is the same—to obey
him: and it is of interest that in the sacrament of baptism that
intention is recognized throughout the whole Church.

These considerations make it clear that in spite of differences, there are many points of likeness, which might well
act as an inspiration to a fuller understanding between the
Churches. The differences are of course not unimportant, and
it would be unwise and even wrong to minimize or to ignore
them. We must accept the fact that every Church has
developed its own traditions over the centuries, and these
traditions are of great value. They bind each generation to its
predecessors, forming an historical unity between past and
present, a continuity in time. But to recognize the fact that
there are many common elements should bring the traditions
closer together to form a continuity across space. A. C.
Outler has put the same point in a slightly different way.

[1] *Catholic Encyclopaedia*, vol. viii, p. 69.   [2] The Scottish Liturgy.

We must recognize a common Christian history. 'The history which separates us from the Event of Christ is also the indispensable nexus which *connects* us with that Event—and thus connects us with each other.'[1]

What constitutes the greatest difficulty is the differences in doctrine. There are very varied views, for example, as to the theology of the eucharistic sacrifice which might seem to make any *rapprochement* almost impossible. Yet it should be recognized that the line of cleavage here is not denominational, and it looks as if even on this point the minds of Christians are not so far apart as they once seemed. The same is true of the problem of the ministry. Different ideas here might seem to limit any progress towards unity, and yet recent conversations, e.g. the Anglican-Presbyterian, the Anglican-Methodist, and the Presbyterian-Congregational, seem to suggest that the problem is not ultimately insoluble. Altogether we should feel that more emphasis should be laid on the common features and less on the differences—never suggesting that the differences do not matter, but certainly in the belief that there must be a way through to an ultimate unity.

Let us now consider some suggestions that have been made for unity through worship. One idea is the holding of selective or eclectic services, where people come together to share in a form which consists of various items chosen from different traditions. These indeed bring worshippers together, but however much they may enjoy the experience, the trouble is that behind the service there is no living tradition. Too often there is no vital connexion between the different elements, and though they may be useful enough for inter-denominational conferences or meetings, they do not really

[1] A. C. Outler, *The Christian Tradition and the Unity we seek* (1958), p. 139.

enlarge the view, nor do they give fuller mutual understanding. Someone has said on this point: 'What is needed is
not a medley but a melodic line, not a patch-work but a
pattern.'[1] Actually it is better, as a rule, to let one denomination have the responsibility for the act of worship, providing
perhaps some explanation of its point of view, its tradition
and its customs.

Another method is to seek for a lowest common de-
nominator. Here is an attempt to bring worshippers together
from many different traditions on the basis of a very simple
doctrinal declaration. The Creed may be dropped, for
example, and perhaps the single phrase, 'Jesus is Lord', sub-
stituted. Let people accept that as the only necessary confession of belief, and let them use their judgement about
everything else. But it is to be feared that a minimal creed of
that nature would not hold people together very long: as we
have already seen, the words mean more than they say. A
specific instance of this is the proposal of Von Ogden Vogt
in his book *The Primacy of Worship*. He holds, rightly, that
worship is the primary concern of the Church and claims
that it alone can have any unitive value. He criticizes all
kinds of dogmatism. 'Dogmas become dogmatism when
they are held to be authenticated by revelation, to be defini-
tive and final, and to be required for religious fellowship.'[2]
That, he holds, keeps people apart. This position, which
suggests a church without any creed or confession, is surely
an anomaly, for the Church has belief as its foundation.
Attempts at corporate church life which rejects the credal, the
sacramental, and the evangelical, will certainly not answer
the problems of unity.

Another suggestion was made by the late Father Raymond

[1] Roger Hazelton, in *Religion in Life*, vol. xix (1949), p. 41.
[2] Von Ogden Vogt, *The Primacy of Worship* (Boston, U.S.A., 1958), p. 63.

Raynes of Mirfield.[1] He proposed not only that in every congregation there should be corporate, silent prayer for the restoration of Christian unity; not only that Christians of various denominations should meet together in their own houses for the same purpose; but that at regular times, say once a month, the bishop of every diocese should himself celebrate the Holy Communion in his cathedral or some central parish church, and all baptized people be invited to attend. At this service the celebrant alone would communicate, or perhaps with a few people with him to satisfy the theological implication of the rubrics. All other members of the church would abstain from receiving, as an act of sorrow and reparation for the sins which had contributed to the disunity of the church, and in common with their brethren of 'separated denominations' who were unable to communicate. One may rejoice in the desire for unity that lies behind this suggestion; but it does seem to emphasize the difficulties about intercommunion, and it is unlikely to prove acceptable to any side.

Again, the Bishop of Woolwich has spoken in favour of a form of concelebration.[2] This touches both the difficulties of ministerial order and of intercommunion, but the interesting thing is the attempt to get over these on an interim plan. He says that in many places, 'we can, and indeed must, spiritually speaking, break one loaf, but . . . we cannot at present do it through a single, mutually acknowledged ministry. Then should we not do it through our divided ministries together? Concelebration with two (or more) ministers presiding at the table on behalf of the congregations they represent, meets those Anglicans who conscientiously believe that it is not a valid eucharist unless celebrated by a priest; and at the same time it accepts as joint celebrant one who is in no way asked

[1] *Thoughts of a Religious* (1959), p. 117.   [2] *Theology*, vol. lxii, Oct. 1959.

to deny the fulness of the ministry he has received' (p. 406). It is not easy to say what the wider reaction to this can be, but it seems to be a plan worthy of consideration and even of experiment.

In conclusion, we may ask: What practical steps can be taken at present, not perhaps for achieving unity, but at least for preparing the road towards it? Recent sad experiments have made it clear that much preparatory work still remains to be done. Let each rebuff, however, only strengthen our determination to make progress towards the desire of our hearts. For we simply *must* find a way together. At this point, however, our worship values should be recognized as having a place in this movement.

There must, of course, be a continuation and an extension of trans-denominational discussion, and that must not be confined to the clergy or to the leaders of the denominations. The discussion must get down to every class, to the office-bearers, to the organizations, to the youth, on all sides. There should be far more occasions when the clergy of one denomination go to meetings of young and of old in another denomination, and there explain their kinds of government, their methods of working, and their ways of worship. There has been some of this, but there must be much more, even in the form of organized campaign.

Again, there must continue united acts of witness where ministers and leaders of various denominations join together and stand by one another in evangelism and on moral and social issues of the day. This is already taking place—the Kirk Weeks in Scotland are an example—but there is need for more of it. Equally important is the need for publicity for these united efforts, drawing the attention of church members, as well as those outside the church, to what is happening.

A good opportunity for members of different denominations getting to know one another is to be found in the house-churches which have come into being in various parts of the country.[1] The original aim of these was evangelism, but development has taken place, so that there are now Bible and prayer groups and also groups containing persons connected more or less closely with different denominations. Here there is clearly opportunity for study not only of the Bible but also of various types of worship, a study which will show not only differences in ethos and method, but also similarities in content and shape where these exist.

The details of worship are also important, however. We have seen how much there is in common in this matter; and the suggestion has been made that that fact should be emphasized. There should be services of worship in which members of different denominations will come together.[2] Attendance at church services to which worshippers are not accustomed must be preceded by explanations, and, if properly prepared for, this would certainly enrich the spiritual experience and help to break down prejudice. The Free Churchman would perhaps be surprised to find that, though he has thought the repetition of Anglican Matins and Evensong week by week (if not day by day) must make the service cold and formal, there are in fact large numbers of people who find in these two services deep spiritual refreshment and enrichment: and the Anglican might also be surprised at the possibility of spiritual refreshment and enrichment in Free Church services, although they depend so much on the mood, the quality and the spiritual attainments of the minister.

A further suggestion is this, that where a service is to be broadcast or televised, arrangements should be made for

[1] See, for example, G. D. Wilkie, *The Eldership Today* (1958); D. C. Orr, *The House Church* (1961); E. W. Southcott, *The Parish Comes Alive* (1956).
[2] Attention might here be drawn to the pamphlet by William Nicholls, *Joining in Common Prayer*, published by the British Council of Churches.

groups to hear the service together, or to gather together after hearing it, for discussion. A minister of the Church responsible for the service should be present to give explanations and answer questions, and generally to help towards the understanding of the service. It might be a good thing for the group to meet before hearing the service, so that its members would be better able to understand what was to be done in the service itself.

There should, moreover, be far more frequent interchange of pulpits, not only on special occasions as in the week of prayer for Christian Unity but on ordinary occasions, so that such exchanges might become a natural and normal thing. In such ways we would get to know each other far better, to understand one another's ideas, and to discover that the really important thing is not the shape of the service, but the worship of the heart offered to Almighty God. This brings us back to what must be regarded as the main bond of unity. Our unity is grounded in the unity of God and in the uniqueness of his redeeming act in Jesus Christ. The Church is one Church, whatever the appearances may suggest, because Christ is one, because he is one for the Church, and because the only true life of the Church is that which it has in him. It is therefore, as one writer puts it, 'not by contrivance or adjustment, that we can unite the Church of God. It is only by coming closer to Him that we can come nearer to one another. And we cannot by ourselves come closer to Him. . . . It will not be by our effort but by His constraining power.'[1] Nevertheless, self-satisfaction, contentment with things as they are, prejudice and complacency, which are only too common in our church life, can put the brake on that constraining power; whereas by attempts at a common worship and understanding such as have been suggested, we

[1] J. J. von Allmen, in *Verbum Caro* (1959), p. 158.

put ourselves in such a position that his power can the more readily and fully act upon us. When we come together in prayer and praise before the eternal throne of God, we are 'caught up into a stream of thanksgiving, the response of the redeemed creature to his Maker, and in the metaphor, so dear to the ancient celebrants, of the crumbs and the loaf, we lose our isolation in assembling and closing in to form the one Bread in Christ'.[1] Without him there is no worship, no Sacrament, no Church. We must plan and continue to plan, though indeed it is not our planning and our diplomatic approaches that will make one body, for in our planning we must recognize his Spirit and his work who hath made both one and hath broken down the middle wall of partition between us, to make in himself of twain one new man, so making peace.

[1] L. V. Powles, *Introduction to the Liturgies of the Anglican Communion* (London, n.d.), p. 30.

EMBODIED WORSHIP

STEPHEN F. WINWARD

'THE whole history of worship might be written round the fascinating and difficult question of the relationship between the outward and the inward.'[1] It is with this relationship that we are concerned in this chapter. Both the outward and the inward are necessarily involved in authentic Christian worship. Why? Because of the nature of God and because of the nature of man. The eternal God whom we worship is revealed and communicated to us through his incarnate Son. 'And the Word became flesh and dwelt among us, full of grace and truth.'[2] Our Christian worship derives its distinctive character from the incarnation of the Word of God. We approach the Father through him in whom 'the complete being of the Godhead dwells embodied'.[3] Nor is this incarnate Word external to the worshippers, for he is the head of the body, the Church. He is the one who includes the many. Christians are in Christ. 'Brought into one body by baptism, in the one Spirit . . . we, many as we are, are one body; for it is one loaf of which we all partake.'[4] It is because we are one body in Christ that we assemble for worship. The congregation of the Lord is the necessary outcome of the incarnation of the Word. Prefigured in the history of Israel and in the synagogue assembly, the

[1] C. F. D. Moule, *Worship in the New Testament* (1961), p. 12.
[2] John i. 14.   [3] Col. ii. 9, N.E.B.
[4] 1 Cor. xii. 13 and x. 17, N.E.B.

congregational worship of the Church is distinctive and unique.

Embodied worship also answers to the nature of man who is not pure, but embodied spirit. 'Thou art man not God, thou art flesh and no angel' (Thomas à Kempis). For this reason worship can never, without serious impoverishment, be 'purely spiritual'. Inner devotion requires outward expression—in words and deeds, in personal and social patterns of activity which include the body, make use of matter, and are perceptible to the senses. The human response to the revelation and communication of God in Christ requires sensible and social embodiment. If the whole personality, 'the body' in the biblical meaning of that phrase, is to be involved in worship, then the inner devotion of the heart must find adequate expression in rite and ceremony, in symbol and sacrament.

The Bible does not set the spiritual over against the material, and does not relegate and confine worship to the former sphere. This is true of both Old and New Testaments. We may take as typical of the Old Covenant the worship offered by David when the Ark of God was first brought into Jerusalem.[1] The Ark itself was the embodied presence; for God was closely associated, if not identified with, that cultic symbol. There was something to be seen; the eyes were involved. So also were the bodies of the worshippers in the solemn procession. The devotion of David was outwardly expressed in the dance. Procession, dance, music, shouting, and song were consummated in sacrifice and sacrament—in the total gift of the burnt offering and the communal feast of the peace offering. All this was very far indeed from being a 'purely spiritual' act of worship. The divine presence and the human response were alike embodied. The Ark, the

[1] 2 Sam. vi.

dance, the offerings, may be taken as representing the three strands which were woven together in the Old Covenant. Symbol, ceremony, and sacrifice were the main constituents of the cult, the embodiment of Hebrew worship.

The crucial words of our Lord to the woman at the well of Sychar are frequently misinterpreted by those who desire to exalt the inward components of worship at the expense of the outward. 'God is spirit, and those who worship him must worship in spirit and in truth.'[1] Approaching this great affirmation with the Hellenistic contrast between the material and the spiritual in mind, it is taken to mean that true Christian worship is immaterial. This is to misinterpret the Bible by means of an alien philosophy. 'Spirit in the Old Testament is regularly not an order of being over against matter, but life-giving, creative activity, and it is in this sense that John commonly uses the word *pneuma*.'[2] God, who takes the initiative in seeking men, is creative and life-giving power, and he is to be worshipped in accordance with his own real or true nature, now disclosed in Jesus Christ. Since the true God is disclosed in the Word made flesh, the response, the true worship, can hardly be disembodied. The worship of the New Covenant, our response to the incarnate God, does not reject sign and symbol, ceremony and sacrament. Two acts, baptism and the Lord's supper, instituted by the Lord himself, were at the heart of primitive Christian worship. Incorporation, and the renewal of life in Christ, were inseparably associated with the material (water, bread, wine), with action (washing, eating, drinking), with symbol, ceremony and sacrament. The enrichment of the inward components of worship in the primitive Church resulted in the simplification, but not the elimination, of the outward.

[1] John iv. 24, N.E.B.
[2] C. K. Barrett, *The Gospel According to S. John* (1955), p. 199.

The material, the enacted, the bodily, all had place and part—kneeling, prostration, the lifting up of hands in prayer, the kiss of peace, baptism, the laying on of hands, the breaking of bread. The Service of the Word—praise, prayer, confession of faith, teaching, prophecy, 'tongues'—was set in the context of the communal meal, of ritual action, of sacrament. In biblical worship, the body (the whole personality) responds to the revelation and communication of the embodied God.

Church history illustrates the tension between the outward and the inward components of worship, and the tendency of Christians to swing to either of two extremes. While the worship of the Church at Rome was, for a long period, concise, austere, and simple, the use of symbols was then carried to extravagant excess in the medieval Church. There was a corresponding elaboration of ceremony—extensive processions and movements, multiplied gestures and bows, crossings, and genuflexions. The reaction against this excessive symbolism, ceremonialism, and externalism at the Reformation was justifiable and not at first extreme. Luther took a middle course, rejecting and simplifying, but also retaining and enriching all such symbols and ceremonies as were not repugnant to the gospel. Calvin, however, reacted in more extreme fashion against the medieval embodiments of worship. The Word of God was enthroned, and the gospel ordinances were stripped of all adornment and action not strictly necessary to their performance. Art and beauty, symbol and image, lights and eucharistic vestments, instrumental music and choirs, gestures and ceremonies, were all alike abolished. It was Zwingli, however, who was the principal opponent of embodied worship. Almost Manichaean in his distinction between the spiritual and the material, he abolished the physical and the sensible, symbol and sacrament (the Lord's supper was retained as an ordinance, not as a means of grace), and relegated worship to the sphere of the mind. This tendency is found in its extreme form in the worship of the Society of Friends. Here the sacraments of baptism and the Lord's supper, together with all sensible things and fixed forms, are alike rejected in favour of an inward spiritual worship. Even at this extreme, however, the necessity for meeting together is recognized, and the sacramental principle is readily acknowledged in life as a whole.

It is important to realize that the post-Reformation reaction against some or many of the outward embodiments of worship was the outcome of intense conviction born of bitter experience. Widespread corruption in Church worship had made the Reformers and their successors keenly aware of the perils of idolatry. There is in some men a strong tendency to become so centred upon and obsessed with symbols and ceremonies, objects and actions, that they fail to pass beyond them to the God they are intended to mediate. Such 'abominable idolatry' is the supreme, but not the only danger accompanying all embodied worship. 'Ritualism' (the attachment of exaggerated or even absolute value to the due performance of ceremony) and formalism (the substitution of the outward performance for genuine personal and corporate devotion) are the age-long foes of worship 'in spirit and in truth'. On the other hand, while understandable, and perhaps inevitable, this hostility to, or suspicion of, the outward embodiments has itself resulted in the creation of an impoverished, distorted, and unbiblical worship. In some traditions the right use (of symbol, ceremony, and sacrament) has been condemned along with the abuse. Within the Reformed (i.e. Calvinist) and the Puritan-Pietist traditions, there has been a powerful reaction against and marked hostility towards embodied worship. Here, all that is addressed to the understanding is 'in', and all appeal to the senses (other than hearing) is 'out'. But this exclusion of the material and the sensuous, of movement and the body, tends inevitably to reduce worship to the exchange of spoken words—whether addressed by God to the people or by the people to God. This weakness is accentuated when the words spoken, in either direction, are largely from the lips of one man. Addressed largely to the understanding, such worship becomes verbose, abstract, intellectualistic, merely notional.

This situation may be illustrated from the worship of a present-day Strict Baptist Chapel—a community in which the Calvinist, Puritan, and Pietist traditions are now mingled and cannot be disentangled. The opening hymn is followed by a long extempore prayer, and the second hymn by the reading of a whole chapter from the Bible. After 'the collection' and another hymn, the sermon is delivered, in length from thirty to forty-five minutes. The service concludes with hymn and benediction. Apart from the collection of gifts, all is verbal; and apart from the hymns, all the words are spoken by one man. The limitations and weaknesses of such a service are obvious. Addressed exclusively to the mind, and making large demands upon the attention, it is not surprising that it makes no appeal to the proletariat in a television age. In the interests of balance, it should also be pointed out that the worship of other Churches is distorted, because they have reacted powerfully against this powerful reaction. Symbol, ceremony, and sacrament have been emphasized at the expense of the centrality of the Word of God, read and preached, and to the exclusion of spiritual freedom and human fellowship in worship. We need biblical wholeness. Affirming the centrality of the Word of God, and the importance of the words of man, we should also seek to involve the eyes and the imagination, the emotions and the sentiments, matter and the senses, the body and its movements. This means, in effect, the full and right use of symbol, ceremony, and sacrament in our services. We shall now look in turn at these three constituents of embodied worship.

A symbol is a representation to the senses of an unseen reality. The symbols used in worship may be divided into auditory and visual—those addressed to the ears and to the eyes respectively. Spoken words are symbols addressed to the ears, and are no exception to the sacramental principle. For in this case meaning and significance are conveyed by the use of a lower medium, the sound waves produced by the human voice. It is worth noting that the distinction between auditory and visual symbols is not absolute. As an eastern proverb puts it: 'He is the eloquent man, who turns his hearer's ears into eyes, and makes them see what he speaks of.' Our Lord himself used picture language, metaphors, parables, stories; he appealed to the imagination, the symbol-forming power within man. The auditory symbol may be addressed to 'the eye of the mind'. Visual symbols, on the other hand, are material objects, designed and shaped by the art and craft of man. The most important of these is the church building itself, which in its design, dignity, simplicity, and beauty should bear eloquent, if silent, testimony to God.

In thinking of church architecture, it is important to get our priorities and sequences right—the incarnation of the Word, the Body of Christ, the local congregation, a building designed for congregational worship. Architecture, especially interior design, can be a hindrance or a help to congregational worship. Like the liturgy, the building should be Christocentric, interior design and arrangement symbolizing the fact that Christ is in the midst of the household of faith. A church should not be a large auditorium with lofty pulpit and galleries. A long-vista building, with lengthy nave, with a chancel behind a screen, and with the Holy Table at the far end against the east wall, is also inimical to corporate worship. God is not 'out there' at the east end; he is present in the Church, the assembly of his people. The sanctuary should be spacious, easy of access, clearly visible, without barrier, and as near to the people as possible. The Lord's Table should be in such a position that the presbyter and his assistants can sit behind it, and the people be arranged immediately in front, or on the other three sides. Whether the building is rectangular or square, round or octagonal, the interior should be so arranged as to keep the whole congregation together, in sight of one another and the central action. It should be designed not only for speaking and listening, but also for movement and action. Since the body can share in worship, there should be facilities for kneeling, as well as for standing and sitting. Central and side aisles should be wide enough for processions. The ritual acts—the entrance of the Bible, the offering of gifts, baptizing, the laying on of hands, the breaking of bread—if the building is rightly designed, will be visible to the congregation, involving eyes as well as ears in worship.[1]

There will also be material symbols within the church building. Of these, the pulpit and the table should be worthy of the centrality of preaching and sacrament. If they are given equal prominence, they will together symbolize the unity of Word and Sacrament in Christian worship. There should also be a worthy symbol of the other great sacrament —baptism. Whether near the entrance or at the centre of the building, font or baptistery should be conspicuous. Even when the word is not being read and preached, and the

[1] For the bearing of the principles of the Liturgical Movement on church architecture, reference may be made to *Towards a Church Architecture* edited by Peter Hammond, and *Outward and Visible* by Basil Minchin.

sacrament is not being celebrated, there is symbolic value in the Large Bible on the lectern, and the paten and cup on the table. A crucifix or an empty cross behind the table, or on the east wall facing the congregation, is an eloquent symbol of the crucified and of the risen Lord. The symbolism of light, taken over by the Church from Jewish domestic worship, has great potency. 'It has certainly been one of the things in the physical environment of man which, from the earliest times we know of, has peculiarly impressed him and been most closely associated with his thoughts of the Divine.'[1] Stained glass, frescoes, framed pictures, statues, may be used to represent the life, death, and resurrection of our Lord. They can also make visible the heroes and saints of the Bible and the Church, and thus help to create an awareness of the communion of saints. Such symbols, 'the books of the unlearned', are much more than 'visual aids' to intellectual understanding; they are, or can be, sacramental. While of special value to children (of all ages!) they should not be despised by any. It is true that as media they may be inferior to verbal symbols. Yet there is no need to sacrifice art in order to appreciate words. 'The Evangelicals, like the Puritans, exalted the ear-gate at the expense of the eye-gate of the soul.'[2] There is no need to continue this one-sided emphasis. Open eyes, as well as open ears, may be engaged in the worship of God.

In turning to the ceremonial element in worship, we are not leaving behind, but extending the application of symbolism. For a symbol is not necessarily a material object; it may be an action. A crucifix is a symbol; so also is the breaking of the loaf. The enacted symbol is more suggestive and potent than the static. Because of the unity of the human

[1] E. Bevan, *Symbolism and Belief* (1938), p. 125.
[2] H. Davies, *Worship and Theology in England*, vol. iii (1961), p. 236.

personality, it is natural that the inner response of the worshipper to God should be expressed in bodily movements and
actions. 'The Hebrew verb most commonly translated "to
worship" (sh-h-h) emphasizes the physical expression appropriate to one who comes into the presence of the holy
majesty of God: he bows himself down, prostrates himself.'[1]
A total response includes the outer as well as the inner. 'O
come, let us worship and *bow down*, let us *kneel* before the
Lord, our Maker.'[2] The appropriate postures for prayer are
standing and kneeling. The Lord stood to pray and assumed
that his disciples would do the same.[3] In Gethsemane, on the
other hand, he knelt, and this posture was frequently adopted
by Christians in the apostolic age—usually in circumstances
of deep emotion or urgent need. Standing is expressive of the
dignity and confidence of the sons of God; kneeling, of
reverence, humility, and submission. In the primitive Church
the prostration of the body (*proskunesis*) was a sign of respect
and submission. Bowing to the symbolic object or to the
symbolic person is an eloquent, if silent, expression of
reverence towards the God thus represented. The hands of
the worshipper veiling the face, or held forth palm to palm,
may express adoring love and loyal allegiance. The ancient
'sacrament of friendship', the kiss of peace, often involved
the clasping of hands; and in some churches today it takes
the form of 'the right hand of fellowship' extended to others.
The presbyter will use his hands in the spontaneous gestures
which accompany preaching; they should also be extended
in greeting, spread forth in intercession, uplifted in blessing.
As in the Old Testament, the solemn procession provides an
opportunity for 'brother ass the body' to participate in
worship. At the beginning of the Service of the Word, the

[1] A. S. Herbert, *Worship in Ancient Israel* (1959), p. 10.
[2] Ps. xcv. 6.   [3] Mark xi. 25.

Bible, carried by an officer of the Church, should precede the minister appointed to read and expound it. This can be an impressive and enacted symbol of the centrality and authority of the Word of God in the assembly. The processional hymn, with choir and minister, or with children and their leaders, is possible in a large church with wide aisles. The offertory, the climax of worship as response, should be made with impressive ceremonial. It should not (as distinct from the collecting of the gifts) be hidden away under cover of a hymn. The congregation should stand as the stewards bring forward the gifts, and these, placed together on one large offertory plate, should be lifted over the Holy Table, and the offertory prayer be said audibly on behalf of the whole company.

It is not possible to discuss here the many ceremonies of the various Christian traditions; our purpose rather is to plead for a balanced combination of rite and ceremony, of that which is said and that which is done. In our Christian worship as a whole, the ceremonial element should be characterized by simplicity, dignity, and clarity. The history of worship clearly shows the twin dangers to be avoided—ceremonial carried to excess and virtually no ceremonial at all. Where it is excessive and over-elaborate, reformation will aim at simplicity and clarity. Where it is lacking, the deficiency must be supplied. For 'the beauty and effectiveness of an otherwise satisfactory service are often marred by deficiencies in necessary ceremonial quite as much as by over-elaboration'.[1]

The third element in embodied worship, the sacraments, we have already been considering in discussing the right use of symbol and ceremony. A sacrament is necessarily both. It is a symbol, an enacted symbol, and yet much more than a symbol. For while a symbol represents, a sacrament conveys.

[1] L. D. Reed, *Worship* (1959), p. 321.

It is true that no hard and fast line can be drawn between symbol and sacrament, for a symbol may be instrumental, may convey the reality it represents, and a sacrament should always represent the reality it conveys. 'Both instrumentality and significance or expressiveness are fundamental constituents of sacramental being, and neither must be made simply adjectival to the other.'[1] Yet in the case of a sacrament, the emphasis falls not upon the picture but upon the act, not upon that which is represented, but upon that which is conveyed. A sacrament is a means of grace, an instrumental symbol, an act of God. In baptism and the eucharist, this act of God is related to the Gospel. For God reveals and communicates himself through his Word, spoken and visible, uttered and embodied, proclaimed by preacher and by Sacrament. It has been and is one of the principal objectives of the Liturgical Movement to restore this unity of Word and Sacrament. For in the history of the Church, the balanced unity of Word and Supper described in the earliest, full, extra-biblical account of the Christian service by Justin Martyr, and characteristic of Church worship in the early centuries, was subsequently lost. The reading of the Scriptures in a language not 'understanded of the people' and the neglect of the preaching of the Word, was followed by a reaction in which the Liturgy of the Word was regarded as a complete service, rarely followed by the Sacrament. When, at the main Sunday service, the Word is invariably consummated in the Sacrament, a local church has taken 'the great leap forward' in the restoration of biblical, embodied worship.

In addition to the unity of Word and Sacrament, there are three other factors in the restoration of embodied worship through the sacraments which may be mentioned—the

[1] O. C. Quick, *The Christian Sacraments* (1927), p. 220.

fellowship, the action, the material. The action of God in the sacraments of baptism and the eucharist is related to the Church, where Christ is present in the midst through the Spirit. Embodied worship presupposes the presence and activity of the Body of Christ, the Fellowship of the Spirit, the Congregation of the Lord. Baptism is not a private ceremony, but initiation into the Body; the eucharist is not 'my communion' but joint-participation in the sacrificed life of Christ. The Congregation of the Lord is not an optional extra. The sacraments are on the way to corruption when separated from either the Word or the Fellowship. The action is also essential—we *do* baptism, we *do* the eucharist. It is through the Fellowship doing the things ordained and commanded with the water, and with the bread and wine, that God's action takes place. It is the bread *we break* and the cup of blessing *we bless* which is a joint-participation in the body and blood of Christ. The stress falls upon the action, *the Church doing* that which Christ has commanded with the material elements. In the eucharist, there is a fourfold action—taking, thanking, breaking, giving. At the conclusion of the Liturgy of the Word, the loaf and the cup, together with the gifts of the people, are carried in solemn procession to the Holy Table, and with offertory prayer placed upon it. Every eucharist is a Harvest Thanksgiving, at which the gifts of God upon which man has laboured are offered to him to become the means of grace. The offertory is followed by the eucharistic prayer, in which by thanking God over the loaf and the cup, they are consecrated to be the communion of the body and blood of Christ. Then comes the third action. Taking the loaf in his hands, and raising it so that it may be seen by all the people, the presbyter breaks bread. It ought not to be, but it is necessary to plead that the service known to the primitive Church as 'the breaking of bread' should include *the action* of breaking bread. The use of manufactured wafers or of tiny sliced cubes of bread is to be deplored. The fourth action is the distribution and consumption of the elements, the communion—whether by the procession of the people to the Holy Table or of the servers to the congregation. Together with the appropriate words, it is by the performance of this fourfold action that we, the Church, 'do the Eucharist'. With reference to the breaking of the loaf, it has already been suggested that we ought not to be afraid of making full use of *the material* of the sacraments. 'God likes matter; he created it' (C. S. Lewis). Are we Gnostics, Manichaeans, or Christian Scientists? Why, for example, are we so afraid of 'our sister water . . . humble, precious, and clean', that we dare only sprinkle a few drops on the forehead of the candidate for baptism? Can such a rite be described as 'the washing of water with the word'?[1] Whether it be by pouring water on the head, or by immersion, let us not be afraid to wash 'with pure water' the bodies of those who are being initiated into the Body of Christ. There can only be a fully embodied worship where the ministers of the Church have overcome their prejudice against dealing with matter! If God likes it, there is no valid reason why we should dislike it.

As illustrating some of the points made above, it may be helpful to outline the weekly Sunday eucharist of one particular Free Church in England which has been influenced by the Liturgical Movement. This service lasts for one hour, and almost the whole congregation stays throughout. Except when reading or preaching, the minister stands or kneels behind the Lord's Table facing the people. The prayers, which may be offered by minister, elder, or deacon, are 'free', i.e. prepared before the service for that one particular

[1] Eph. v. 26.

service. The whole has three main parts—the Preparation, the Service of the Word, the Supper. The Preparation consists of a scriptural Call to Worship; a Hymn of Praise; a Call to Penitence, Confession of Sin and Assurance of Pardon; a Prayer of Supplication; the Collection of the gifts of the people which are retained at the rear of the church; the Notices for the week. The Service of the Word may begin with a hymn, and includes the Old Testament, the Epistle, a metrical or prose Psalm, the Gospel, the Sermon, the Prayers of Intercession and the Lord's Prayer. This is followed by 'the fencing of the Table', i.e. an Invitation to the Lord's Supper with a clear statement of the conditions for participation. This ends the Service of the Word, and during a few moments of organ music, the elders and deacons join the minister behind the Table, and those who so desire, leave. Then follows the fourfold action of the eucharist. Following Offertory Sentences, the people stand as the gifts are brought forward by the stewards and dedicated to God in prayer—the elements to be a means of grace to those present, the money for the work of the Kingdom of God in the world. A Hymn, Communion Sentences, and a Prayer of Approach introduce the Prayer of Thanksgiving—the Adoration of the Father, the Commemoration of the Son, the Invocation of the Spirit, the Oblation of the worshippers. The third action, the Breaking of Bread, takes place as the Words of Institution are recited. After serving the minister, the deacons deliver the bread and the wine to the people. A brief Prayer of Thanksgiving, the *Nunc Dimittis*, *Te Deum* or Hymn, and the Blessing conclude the service.

If there is to be a total act of worship, the whole personality of man must be involved in the response to the revelation and communication of God through Christ the incarnate Word. It cannot be total if certain aspects of the whole personality are excluded, or at least inadequately expressed. The senses must not be banned, the body must not be excommunicated. Traditions of worship predominantly verbal, notional, intellectual, must be so reformed that the sentiments and the senses, movement and action, matter and the body, are also included and involved. The false antithesis between the spiritual and the material, the soul and the body, must be overcome, if we are to recover biblical wholeness. The inward and the outward components of worship must not by man be put asunder, for God himself has joined them together.

PRAYER—
FIXED, FREE AND EXTEMPORARY

JOHN HUXTABLE

IT is well to define terms as clearly as possible; and a distinction needs to be drawn between a liturgy in which form and content are prescribed, as in the Roman *Missal* and in the *Book of Common Prayer*; a directory in which form is defined and precise content left to the discretion of the minister, as in Presbyterian *Books of Common Order*; and types of worship in which both the former are eschewed, since minister and people depend on the immediate guidance of the Holy Spirit, as with the earlier Separatists and the Quakers generally. 'Liturgy' can be used to describe all forms of corporate worship; and those most addicted to set forms of prayer could not agree that their worship is unrelated to the Holy Spirit. Moreover the prayer offered in Baptist or Congregationalist worship is frequently based on previous consideration and preparation. In *A Guide to Prayer* (1715) Isaac Watts makes a distinction between free prayer and extemporary prayer. Free or 'conceived' prayer is prepared before the service; it is 'done by some work of meditation before we begin to speak in prayer'. Extemporary prayer is spontaneous and unpremeditated—'when we without any reflection or meditation beforehand address ourselves to God and speak the thoughts of our hearts as fast as we conceive them'. The difference between conceived and extemporary prayer is, however, one of degree, since there may be much, some, little or no preparation in advance. It is not therefore easy to decide to what extent prayer in the Free Churches is extemporary. For all the truth in these qualifications, however, these broad distinctions between liturgy, directory and extemporaneity are broadly true.

It is important to observe that by no means all those who conscientiously objected to the 1662 Prayer Book were liturgical anarchists. Indeed, some of them objected to the Book more because of the manner of its imposition on the Church than because of the type of worship enjoined; and those who had deeper theological grounds for their objection were not blind to the importance of form in the public worship of God. John Knox's *Forme of Prayers 1556*, used while Knox was minister of the English congregation of Marian exiles in Geneva, 1556–9, had considerable influence, by no means only in Scotland. Forms of service are provided therein, and what may be called 'model' prayers are also provided; but it is clear that they are not obligatory. For example, the form of prayer for the Sunday Morning Service begins with the injunction: 'when the congregation is assembled, at the houre appointed, the minister useth one of these two confessions, *or lyke in effect*'.[1] Similar injunctions occur frequently, and serve to illustrate the fact that the precise content put into the form was left to the discretion of the minister. *The Book of the Forme of Common Prayers*, published by Waldegrave in 1554 or 1555, and a book with a similar title used by Puritan exiles at Middleburgh (1586, 1587 and 1602) are part of the evidence that Knox's service book exercised a powerful influence on English Church life; so also do the *Parliamentary Directory* (1644) and the *Savoy*

[1] W. D. Maxwell, *John Knox's Genevan Service Book, 1556* (Edinburgh, 1931), p. 85 (my italics).

Liturgy of 1661. Indeed, the aim of a directory can hardly be more exactly described than in the preface to the *Parliamentary Directory*; 'our meaning therein being only that, the general heads, the sense and the scope of the prayers, and other parts of worship being known to all, there may be a consent of all the Churches in those things that contain the substance of the service and worship of God'; and the aim of this manual—it was clearly not intended as a prescribed form—was that by it ministers may 'if need be, have some help and furniture, and yet so as they become not hereby slothful and negligent in stirring up the gifts of Christ in them; but that each one, by meditation, by taking heed to himself and the flock of God committed to him, and by wise observing of the ways of Divine Providence, may be careful to furnish his head and tongue with further and other materials of prayer and exhortation, as shall be needful upon all occasions'.[1]

Horton Davies's book, *The Worship of the English Puritans* refers to the objections to set forms which were held by the Barrowists and the Brownists and those who followed in their tradition, among whom were John Owen and Isaac Watts. It was John Owen who regarded the imposition of liturgies as 'the gilding of the poisonous pill, whose operation when it was swallowed, was to bereave men of their sense, reason, and faith'. It is not to be wondered, therefore, that the first of the objections Horton Davies enumerates is that set forms of prayer were thought to deprive a minister of the gift of prayer; to which there is added that such forms cannot meet the needs of varied congregations and occasions, that they lead people to suppose that God could not be worshipped in any other way, that they conduce to hypo-

---

[1] Hall, *Reliquiae Liturgicae*, iii. 18 ff. and 115 ff. This whole theme is dealt with at length in Horton Davies, *The Worship of the English Puritans* (1948).

crisy, and that the imposition of them has led to persecution.[1] It is fair to say that there combined with these objections a fear lest the Spirit be quenched and a dread lest worship become dead and formal. These may not present an unanswerable case, but they state concerns which may not be dismissed out of hand, since they represent the convictions of a large number of Christians, among whom the Pentecostalist groups must now be added to the more historic Protestant Churches already mentioned. It must, however, be said as well that historic Dissent has continually felt the influence of the 'directory type' of worship even when it has been most emphatic about extemporaneity. Perhaps Isaac Watts is typical of such: he held that 'the perpetual confinement of ourselves to a form . . . renders our converse with God very imperfect. Since new temptations and new wants should be taken up into our prayers and new sins confessed, it is not to be thought that these can be well provided for in any pre-scribed composition.'[2] So he advocates avoiding 'these two extremes: I. A confining of ourselves to precomposed forms of prayer. II. An entire dependence on sudden motions and suggestions of thought.'[3]

It is important to notice that even the freest sort of worship is rarely without form; indeed, the most enthusiastic advo-cates of freedom in worship are often careless in their claims, since they rely more upon forms of worship than they would readily admit, and are sometimes extremely con-servative about such forms of worship as they have. If we take the Quakers as the example of complete liturgical freedom, we must reckon them so exceptional as to be unique. For the rest, even the most radical Protestants have a recognizable pattern of worship. They are not and they do

[1] Op. cit., pp. 98 ff.
[2] Isaac Watts, *Guide to Prayer; Works* (1810), vol. iv, p. 27.
[3] Op. cit., p. 127.

not wish to be free from the Bible and the sacraments, though they would resist in many cases the use of a lectionary and reject 'ritualistic' observances of the sacraments. The freedom claimed is largely confined to the prayers and to 'liberty of prophesying'. If we read such accounts as we have from contemporary sources of Puritan worship, a common form is quite recognizable.[1] It is interesting to observe further that when the precise order of such worship is listed item by item, the family likeness of all Christian worship is made perfectly plain, a point which becomes quite clear to anyone who has carefully compared the Order of the Mass in the *Missal* with the Order of Holy Communion in the *Book of Common Prayer* and both of these with the forms provided from time to time by Baptists, Congregationalists and Presbyterians. It may be noted here that Methodism is in an interestingly mediating position. The forms of sacramental worship in its *Book of Offices* are virtually identical with the Anglican forms. These are, it seems, very extensively used in Methodism. The suggested form of Morning Prayer (also virtually identical with that of Anglicanism) is not so commonly used, for in non-sacramental worship Methodism has more and more used forms of worship typical of the other English Free Churches. This ought to mean that Methodism could be in a particularly advantageous position to indicate ways in which free and liturgical worship may be combined.

Watts's objection to 'precomposed forms' did not, however, apply to hymns, which, as has been pointed out by many writers, have a peculiar value in the worship of most Reformed Churches, though here again the Quakers are an exception; and no consideration of free and set forms of worship can be complete without recognizing that in historic

[1] Cf. Horton Davies, op. cit., pp. 162 ff. and 204 ff. See also A. G. Matthews, 'The Puritans' in *Christian Worship*, ed. N. Micklem (Clarendon Press, 1936); and H. M. Dexter, *A Handbook of Congregationalism* (Boston, 1880), pp. 42–62.

Dissent as well as in Methodism the hymn book has had a place in the life of devotion only comparable with that of the *Book of Common Prayer* in the life of an Anglican. Of the use of the hymn book in private devotion it is not now relevant to write; but it is very much to the point to remark that in the worship of the directory or extemporary type hymns have an extremely important position. They are not only the vehicle for the people's praise; they are also its way of confessing its faith and expressing its convictions and aspirations. Moreover, they provide the people's part in the dialogue of worship. To say that such forms of worship too often leave the worshipper passive and unduly dominated by the person who is leading worship may be in some measure true; but such a characteristic vice could only arise from abuse; and it is only when the function of the hymn in worship is misunderstood or underestimated that the charge can be made to stand: and in this most characteristic feature of worship 'precomposed forms' are essential: it is in order to ask why it is thought right to use another's words in praise and not in prayer.

At the beginning of this chapter it was remarked that the threefold distinction drawn between the main types of Christian worship was only very rough and ready; and we must now observe that in recent times it is being made increasingly unsatisfactory. One of the tokens of liturgical renewal is dissatisfaction with what is 'merely' traditional and a corresponding desire to discover what riches may be available from other traditions. One relatively small, but not unimportant, indication of this has been the very general Anglican desire to experiment 'after the third collect'. Numbers of books of prayers have appeared which aim at providing clergymen with useful material by which the intercessions of the people may be enriched. It would be interesting to know to what extent, if any, free or extemporary prayer could be given a place in Matins or Evensong after the third collect: what is clear is that, when the officiating minister calls upon the people to pray for this or that matter according to the needs of the occasion or according to the general needs of mankind, and uses some *ad hoc* words in which to express such prayer, he is moving a long way towards a 'directory', if not an extemporary, form of worship.

At the same time there is a corresponding readiness on the part of many Free Churchmen to experiment with different liturgical forms and to set greater value than previously upon what are sometimes called set forms. Occasionally this takes the form of piecemeal and not very intelligent borrowing from the *Book of Common Prayer*; and in such an eccentric book as W. E. Orchard's *Divine Service* (O.U.P., 1926) dissatisfaction with dissenting forms of worship finds expression in the sort of borrowing from other liturgical traditions which has little understanding of one's own. More recently there has been a growing appreciation of the Christian Year and an increasing willingness to understand and to put into practice 'native' liturgical principles, and, when appropriate, to learn from other traditions. It is no longer true, as once it was, that Free Church scholars do not write upon liturgical subjects; and the various service books put out by the Free Churches not only indicate this renewed liturgical interest but reflect also the scholarly work of some of their ministers. There is no scope in this brief chapter to describe in detail what is contained in these books; but some of them may be listed. It should be noted that not all of them have official standing; but all of them have been widely used. The *Book of Common Order* (1928), the *Book of Common Order* (1940), *Prayers for the Christian Year* (1935, and a revised and expanded edition 1952), have been published by the Church of Scotland and have had wide influence beyond Scotland and beyond Presbyterianism. English and Welsh Presbyterians published *The Presbyterian Service Book* in 1948. A group of Congregationalists published *A Book of Public Worship* in 1948; and the Revd. J. M. Todd, a Congregational minister, published *Prayers and Services for Christian Festivals* in 1951; and a *Book of Prayers and Services* was published by the Congregational Union of England and Wales in 1959. In addition to their *Book of Offices* the Methodist Church published *Divine Worship* in 1935. In 1958 among the Baptists the Revd. S. F. Winward published *Responsive Praises and Prayer*, and together with Dr. E. A. Payne, Mr. Winward also brought out *Orders and Prayers for Church Worship* in 1960. This is a typical rather than a complete list, which indicates a movement affecting all the major Free Churches.

If it be asked what has caused this renewal of interest in liturgy, a major part of the answer is to be found in the fact that the Free Churches have been affected by the liturgical revival which is manifest in all the Churches; and the wider contacts made possible through the Ecumenical Movement have aroused interest in ways of worship not only in Churches of this country but in others as well. For example, the work of Lutheran and Reformed Churches on the Continent as well as of Romans and Anglicans has been studied and taken into account. Liturgical scholars have not only looked again at the beginning of their own traditions, but they have been driven to ask what there is to be learned from other traditions and whether their own tradition is exclusive of others. A mutual enrichment has already begun and, it may be hoped, will increase; but learning from another tradition is always a delicate operation, since liturgical practice reflects theological conviction: the question must always be asked: What theological and religious overtones does this liturgical practice assume?

The Free Churches are more ready to enter upon this process of learning and experiment since there has been and is among them considerable discontent with the sort of worship common at the beginning of this century and still prevailing in some quarters. Was it adequate? Was it sufficiently alive? Did it truly correspond to the Gospel? Was it needful to abandon colour, movement, dialogue as completely as had hitherto been supposed? More than that, the question some people[1] raised of the 'psychological' difficulty of free prayers as against 'known' forms. Whereas it is a psychologically difficult threefold exercise to grasp the free prayer of the minister, make it your own and direct it to God, it is relatively 'easier' if the form of words is known. It is, of course, true that familiar words can become so well known that they make their own demand on concentration if they are not to become an idle rote; but, aware of this danger, some Free Churchmen asked whether some set forms might not be usefully incorporated into the worship they were required either to lead or to attend.

A number of different factors, therefore, have contributed to create a situation in which presuppositions are being examined and traditions rediscovered and questioned, in which experiments are being made and enrichment sought. No longer are free prayer and set forms of prayer seen as mutually exclusive; and we may hope that we shall all discover a liturgy which is truly catholic because it is not only traditional but also because it gathers into a living whole all that Christ's people have discovered about ways of worship.

[1] e.g. E. R. Micklem, *Our Approach to God* (1934), pp. 162 ff.

PRIVATE DEVOTION

RUPERT E. DAVIES

ALL Christians recognize the need for private devotion as
well as for corporate worship—or shall we say, almost all
Christians; for there are said to be some members of Scan-
dinavian Lutheran Churches who hold that private prayer is to
be discouraged, lest it lead to the notion that we are justified
by what we do—in this case, saying our prayers. The problems of private devotion are not so much theoretical as
practical; we do not have to argue for the value of it, but so
to order our lives that there is time for it, and the present
writer has good personal reasons for knowing how difficult
this is. But perhaps the difficulty of such problems would be
lessened if we were clearer in our minds as to what it is that
we are doing when we pray by ourselves or in our families
and knew what various methods of private prayer are found
valuable and helpful by those who use them.

We tend—even the most devout among us, and perhaps
most of all the most devout of us—to regard our own prayers
in private as distinct from the prayers of the Church as a
whole; they form a stream of devotion which runs parallel
with, but never meets or joins, the corporate prayer of the
Church. We even sometimes find ourselves in the position of
preferring our own private prayers to those which we hear said
in church, on the grounds that they are more personal and
sincere than those which are said for us by someone who

cannot possibly know our intimate needs, and that the worship of a congregation is cold, lifeless and formal in comparison with the warmth and intensity of our personal prayer-time. If we feel like this, it must be that we are thinking that congregational worship should be a collection of private interviews with God—which is very different from its nature as defined in this book. But such feelings, even if we do not entertain them for long, and try to banish them from our mind, show that we regard public prayer in church and private prayer at home as two quite different and unrelated activities.

In actual fact this is not the case. Our private prayers are an extension of our prayers in church. Even if we utter our prayers in a place remote from every gathering of God's people, we are still praying with God's people; when we pray at home, or in the middle of our daily work, we are praying with the Church—and not only with the other members of the congregation to which we belong, or with the other members of the denomination to which we belong, but with the Holy, Catholic Church on earth and in heaven. It is natural that in our times of private devotion we should lift up to God our own personal, private and family needs, rather more than we are likely to be able to do in church; but we do this, surely, in the context of the whole Church's prayer for all its members. We never pray *for* ourselves only, or at least never except in times of desperate need; for we are members of each other, and every need of our own involves others, and every need of others involves ours. Nor do we ever pray *by* ourselves only, because 'the voice of prayer is never silent', and the Church is always at prayer somewhere and our prayers are taken up into the prayers of the whole Church: and even if it were true that at some particular time no one on earth was praying except us, the Church in heaven, which is the same Church, would certainly be praying with us and for us. So the Christian at prayer is never alone and need never feel himself to be alone. His togetherness with the whole Church should never be simply implicit and taken for granted, and therefore often forgotten; it should come out in the way he prays and the methods he uses. This point becomes very plain when we remember that when we pray we have to use, very often, the prayers already prayed by others. Unless we are saints, our spiritual resources are certain to be so meagre that if we had to rely on them alone for the substance and words of our prayers, those prayers would be poor and narrow indeed: and if we are saints, we shall not dream of relying on ourselves in such a way (if we may judge from the testimony of those who are known to be saints).

All prayer, then, is with and in the Church, however 'private' it may be. This is somewhat clearer in 'family prayers', but it is just as true at other times. In an earlier generation—perhaps thirty or forty years ago—'family prayers' were almost the most characteristic part of the Christian way of life in Great Britain. This is certainly no longer the case. It is impossible to obtain an accurate account of the present situation; but it is highly probable that 'family prayers' are now very rare indeed, although some families who have given up the practice on week-days resume it on Sunday, as the only day on which the family can come together in reasonable quietness of spirit. But even this is far from common, and the fact is that 'family prayers' are a casualty of modern life for ordinary Christians. The traditional long Bible reading, followed by the even longer extemporary but comprehensive prayer (with suitable animadversions on the current state of the world and the family), had become somewhat meaningless and tedious to many

Christians long before the practice died out; and where 'family worship' still takes place, it usually takes the form of a short Bible reading according to some prescribed lectionary, often with comments read from the notes provided by the compilers of the lectionary, followed by a short prayer in direct relation to national and personal needs. The stage of development which a family has reached (viz. the numbers and age of the children) will largely determine whether such a practice is possible, but it is probably more often possible than actual. Many families could, if they had a mind, consider establishing it at least on a weekly basis, and even if the children could not be included for various reasons of absence, age, attitude to religion, and the like, husband and wife together could constitute the family for this purpose. This does, of course, frequently happen. We shall see later whether such family prayers could include rather more of the ingredients of worship than they normally do and at the same time remain brief and concise.

Most often, probably, private devotions are individual—and therefore the need of reminder that all prayer is in and with the Church is all the more necessary. It is the duty of every Anglican clergyman to say the Offices of Morning and Evening Prayer every day. This obligation has for them immense advantages which we need not discuss; but there *are* dangers of formality, and the length of the Offices make them difficult for lay-people to use. The great standby of lay-people has been for many years the schemes of Bible reading with notes provided by the Bible Reading Fellowship, the International Bible Readers' Association and the Scripture Union. In practice, the B.R.F. notes have proved more congenial to Anglicans, those of the I.B.R.A. to Free Churchmen, and those of the S.U. to those who accept the literal inspiration of Scripture. The reasons for this in the last case are clear enough and have to be accepted; in the other two cases the reasons are not particularly obvious or strong. The various series of notes are graded to suit the needs of different age-groups, and a high level of writing and biblical understanding has been consistently maintained, although it has at times been possible to wonder whether the notes could not perhaps be made more attractive to those people not versed in the ways and thoughts of the Church. It is quite clear that this method fulfils a very great need. Bible reading without notes—especially if it takes the form of going through the Bible book by book—can be a soul- and mind-destroying occupation; and it is the more deplorable in an age in which scholarly knowledge has thrown a great deal of light on the meaning of Scripture, not only for the biblical expert, but also for the humblest believer.

The use of hymns for the purposes of meditation in private devotion is not as extensive as it might be. Not all hymns, of course, are suitable; but on the whole those that are least appropriate for congregational singing because of their intimate character are most appropriate for our present purpose. Many generations of Methodists have found the hymns of Charles Wesley especially congenial; but there is nothing specifically Methodist about them, and it is on record that at least one member of the Anglican Society of St. Francis used a hymn of Charles Wesley every day for devotional purposes for a period of his life.

Books of meditation are legion; each of us must look for the one that is most helpful and be willing to pass on to another when the value of the first has been exhausted. This is not, alas, as easy as it sounds. A large proportion of such books have the same general characteristics which appeal to those Christians who have a deep affection for the traditional analyses of the human soul and the ancient forms of Christian observance; and these Christians are therefore abundantly catered for. Other Christians, however, whose minds are cast in a different mould and come from other traditions, often find these books virtually unusable, and have very little else to help them. This situation is gradually being dealt with by the various communions; and there is, for example, a useful bibliography of small books for private devotion in a leaflet issued jointly by the Congregational Union of England and Wales and the Presbyterian Church of England under the title of *When you pray, say* . . .[1]

Numerous collections and selections of prayers have been published in recent years, some of which are extremely good. Those likely to be most useful contain a number of prayers under the headings of Adoration, Thanksgiving, Confession, Intercession, and Petition (or similar titles), and include prayers from all parts and periods of the Church. Ancient prayers which are still in use justify themselves, not for antiquarian reasons, but because they have proved their value to many generations of Christians; they have the additional merit of bringing home to the modern man the continuity of the Church throughout the ages. There is no need to stress the value of prayers from the *Book of Common Prayer*, or from the pens of great Christians of the past. Probably too many prayers written in English during the nineteenth century prove on examination to be merely imitative of an older style and to be somewhat thin in content, sonorous though they often are: but some of them can still be used with profit. Modern prayers will always cause contention (the older ones, when they were modern, did the same). Nevertheless, those which are not turgid or fanciful may often em-

---

[1] At present (1965) obtainable from 217 Memorial Hall, Farringdon Street, London, E.C.4, at 1*d*.

body our needs and those of our contemporaries far better than the older prayers can possibly do.

No sensible Christian will despise the richness, the breadth and the depth which can be given to his praying by the prayers of others whose needs differ from what he believes to be his own and whose tradition and vision may even seem to conflict with his: but there is still a poverty about our prayers unless we have learned to add something of our own, meagre and inadequate though it may seem to us to be. This means, perhaps above all, that we must learn to be silent in the presence of God, that he may speak to us: for some of us this is most unpleasantly hard. It also means that we must learn to pray in our own words—maturely, if we are mature Christians, and not nostalgically in the words of childhood. This will happen only if we have understood that our whole life is, in one sense, our prayer; and that uttered or thought prayer is the overflowing of our life into words—the intensification of that relationship with God which is the essence of our Christian faith. Private prayer is fully real only when this happens; and it happens only if we apply ourselves to private prayer in the serious resolve to make it, with God's help, what it should be. This may mean serious effort over a long period.

There is undoubtedly a great variety in practice among those who continue the habit of private prayers, and some people may think it desirable that this variety should continue. It is apparent, however, that all the methods that are used contain weaknesses—some are too introspective; some go too far the other way; some consist only of extemporary prayer, some only of set prayer; some leave the Bible out; some concentrate wholly on Bible reading; some find no place for one or other of the fundamental elements in worship—adoration, thanksgiving, confession, intercession, petition; and all tend to belong to one 'tradition' or another. Has not the time come when we may contemplate the drawing up of 'Daily Offices' which could be used by members—families and individuals—of all traditions and all communions? They could be available for ministers and lay-people alike, though no doubt lay-people would usually use a shortened form. They would need both to be variable, in case Free Churchmen suspect them of undue rigidity, and to contain traditional elements, so that Anglicans might not be put off by a break with the past; and, of course, a combination of the variable and the traditional is valuable in itself. They would need to contain all the integral elements of worship, even if in a brief form, and could no doubt embody them into a fourfold pattern of Praise, Bible Reading, Penitence and Prayer. Psalmody, selected and in many cases abbreviated, would of course find a place, and it could be used for praise or penitence or petition, according to its content. A canticle would be the natural vehicle of praise, but a hymn might sometimes take its place; or a hymn could be used for penitence or prayer. One or more passages of Scripture would come into each Office; perhaps in the morning a reading from both Old and New Testaments, and in the evening one from the New Testament only. No doubt a short comment from some source would be needed. In these ways large parts of the Bible could be read through fairly continuously. The Offices could all be 'open-ended'—that is to say, there would be suggested set prayers, but also a place for silence, and the addition of personal extemporary prayers according to the needs and the concerns of the individual.

Such Offices would combine the best elements in many traditions. They have yet to be drawn up, and would fulfil their true purpose completely only if they gained general acceptance. But if they did gain such acceptance, they would be of real assistance to many individual Christians who wished to pray with the Church, and they would help to bring Christians whose communions are still separated from each other into a real and growing unity.

LITURGY AND THE MISSION
OF THE CHURCH

R. ALED DAVIES

'A CHURCH which is inward-looking', says Joost de Blank, 'is really no church at all.'[1] A church which is inward-looking is a church which has become concerned with itself; and because it has become introverted it has lost the main characteristic of the Church of the New Testament, its concern for the world. Another way of saying the same thing is to say that a church which has turned in on itself is a church which has lost its sense of mission.

One reason why a church gets into this state is that for some people religion is an escape from reality. For them the Church is a kind of ghetto withdrawn from the main life of the community and they use it as a refuge from the world; instead of trying to convert the world, they try to escape from it; and so the Church is not a place from which to launch an attack but a comfortable place to which to retreat. That is why, to many people in the world around us, religion appears, not as dynamic revolutionary belief but as an escape route from the pressures of life. Another more subtle form of the same attitude is the confusion in the minds of church people between mission and activity. Many church members are prepared to spend time and energy promoting a vigorous church life; for them the well-attended meeting on some

[1] Joost de Blank, *The Parish in Action* (1954), p. 16.

quite secular subject like 'My holiday in San Sebastian' and the existence of a multiplicity of clubs and societies within the church have become ends in themselves. As long as there is plenty going on they ask no questions. But the Church is not an end in itself; it exists to carry out a missionary task and one of the easiest ways of avoiding that obligation is to involve ourselves in a whirlwind of church organizations. Some of the more sceptical onlookers have gone so far as to say that when the Church has shown some interest in the world by conducting campaigns for revival, crusades, visitation evangelism and the like, it has done so, not because it cares fundamentally for the world and its people but because it sees them as potential church members and having got them 'into the Church' and subscribing towards the upkeep of the institution they have served their purpose. People are not valuable in themselves, they are only valuable as 'pew fodder'.

Against such a background it is essential to assert over and over again that the object of God's love is the *world*. God's love is not restricted to the few, 'the elect', but goes forth to the whole of mankind. It embraces every kind of person following every kind of occupation, men and women of all nationalities and of all conditions, creeds and colours. To each the love of God goes out in equal measure and of each it remains true that 'underneath are the everlasting arms'. The Christian believes that this concern for mankind is to be seen in the record of God's activity in the world as it is found in the Bible. The Scriptures, having shown that God created the world and saw 'that it was very good'.[1] goes on to narrate the story of man's rebellion against him. Intended by God to live in Paradise, in perfect freedom and innocence, man, by his rejection of God's plan, forfeited his place, lost

[1] Gen. i. 31.

his real freedom and innocence and knew the guilt and shame that comes from sin. Made for existence with God, he continually turns from it. Because he refuses to be his true self, man lives as less than himself and commits those sins which have ever been a blot on his name. Beginning with the murder of Abel, fallen man has turned his hand against his brother and his history is the record of violence, bloodshed, deceitfulness and inhumanity.

Having given us a prologue describing man's plight the Bible goes on to record God's rescue operations, beginning with the choice of Abraham. But in spite of leader, priest and prophet, the Israelites failed to live up to their calling and in the end God sent his Son, who is both the image of God and the one true Israelite, to reveal to man the love of God and to offer that perfect obedience which the people of God had failed to give. In Christ we see what man ought to be: we see what a '*real human*'—a human not corrupted by sin—is like. Here is a true Son of God, not only because he comes from God but also because in him we see what real filial obedience and love are like. This second Adam, who was to restore what the first Adam had lost, was faced by the twin enemies of sin and death—and in order to establish a bridgehead into the human situation these must be defeated. This Christ did. Subjected to temptations he did not succumb, faced with the agony of death he prayed only that his Father's will might be done, and when his sufferings on the Cross brought death near he could yield himself to his Father in the words: 'It is finished.' The bonds which held humanity in thrall had been broken and the victory achieved. By this victory the 'break through', as it might be described, had been made. The image lost in Adam is now restored in Jesus Christ. This lodgement by 'Man' as he is truly meant to be within the world of 'men' provides the spearhead for a thrust for-

ward to recover the lost ground and to bring ever-increasing
numbers into the fold of this 'new creation', this New
Humanity, of which Christ is the Head. This new creation
is to be Christ's Body in the world, a description used by
the New Testament writers to describe the nature of the
Church.

But how does a man become part of this Body? The
Scriptural answer is that he cannot simply join it as if he were
committing himself to a political party or paying a sub-
scription to belong to a club. Christians sometimes seem to
act like that; but the political party demands no radical
transformation in the man, whereas the Christian Church
does. It can only be open to those who are prepared to undergo death. This death to self is in fact the gateway to the new
life and it is symbolized by the ritual by which a person becomes a member of the church—the sacrament of baptism.
As practised in New Testament times baptism was normally
by total immersion. The body of the person was submerged
below the water as if he were being lowered into the grave;
it was the symbol of death. Being raised to the surface was
likewise the symbol of resurrection to the 'new life in Christ'.
By this action, described for us in the sixth chapter of
Romans,[1] the 'old man' is dead and the 'new man'[2] is
incorporated or made one with Christ himself and also, by
that very fact, made one with the visible Body of Christ,
his Church.

There are many ways by which St. Paul describes this
experience: the use of the figure of the 'new man', the
declaration 'ye are not your own but are bought with a
price',[3] the statement which he makes with regard to himself, 'Paul, a slave of Christ',[4] or the similar phrase which he

---

[1] Rom. vi. 6; cf. Eph. iv. 22; Col. iii. 9.
[2] 2 Cor. v. 17; Gal. vi. 15; Eph. ii. 15 and iv. 24.
[3] 1 Cor. vi. 20; vii. 23.   [4] Rom. i. 1; Phil. i. 1.

uses to underline his relationship with Christ, 'whose I am and whom I serve',[1] or again 'for me to live is Christ'.[2] All these say in different words that the apostle is now the very possession of Christ and that his life consists in doing the will of Christ. In so doing he has not lost his freedom but is now truly free; in so losing his life the very life of Christ flows into him.[3] As Teilhard de Chardin has said, 'Union with Christ presupposes essentially that we transpose the ultimate centres of our existence into him—which implies the radical sacrifice of egoism.'[4]

Here then is the Church; a body of men and women who by death to themselves are incorporated into Christ and now live a new life in him. In this process the new man recovers his lost status and in virtue of this he becomes truly human because now he is truly God's. Here is restored humanity, humanity as it ought to be, humanity in all its new-found freedom, emancipated from the false group loyalties of colour, class and nation (and in the divided church it might be added—denomination) which imprison man. Echoes of this reach us from the pages of the New Testament. The Acts of the Apostles tell us how, as Peter spoke to the crowd after Pentecost, the very barrier of language was broken down as if the primal unity of man had been restored.[5] Paul the Pharisee, proud with the pride of one of the spiritual élite of Judaism, tells us that 'For as many of you as were baptized into Christ did put on Christ. There can be neither Jew nor Greek, there can be neither bond nor free, there can be no male and female: for ye all are one man in Christ Jesus.'[6] This international characteristic of the Church is not simply because the Church is to be found in every part of the world, for at the beginning this was not so; nor is it

---

[1] Acts xxvii. 23.   [2] Phil. i. 21.   [3] Gal. ii. 20.
[4] T. de Chardin, *Le Milieu Divin*, p. 93.   [5] Acts ii. 1-12.
[6] Gal. iii. 27, 28.

because it has achieved this in the succeeding centuries. It is because right at its very heart the Church is trans-national. It reaches below the artificial and accidental groupings of mankind to the basic humanity latent in us all and calls upon us to be what we were created to be and which by death and resurrection in Christ we can be.

The Church exists in order to bring this new humanity into being. When the Church turns in upon itself as if the world were not its concern, then, of necessity, it cannot fulfil its mission; for the very material of which the new humanity is made lies 'out there' in the world waiting to be transformed.

II

If this is the task given to the Church, the question that must be asked is: 'How does the Church carry it out?' The answer is that it carries out its mission according to the pattern given by Jesus Christ. That pattern might well be described as the pattern of Incarnation and Suffering.

A

The Incarnation

Many Christians, in talking about their faith, isolate the Cross as if it were not really connected with what had gone before. No one would dispute the centrality of the Cross in the Christian faith and in the life and experience of individual Christians. Christian hymns and writings over the centuries make that abundantly clear. But the Cross stands out in its uniqueness because of something which took place before it, the Incarnation. Crucifixion was a common occurrence in the Roman Empire and there was nothing in the eyes of the world to distinguish the central cross of the three on Calvary from the other two. The difference between the crucifixion of Christ and the other crucifixions was not simply that Christ was innocent and the others were guilty, but because the other victims were men while Christ was both God and man. Christ was the 'Word made flesh'.[1] Quietly, unobtrusively, he who was God slipped into the world at Bethlehem. As St. Paul describes it in his great passage in the Epistle to the Philippians, 'Jesus Christ, being in the form of God, counted it not a prize to be on an equality with God, but emptied himself, taking the form of a servant, being made in the likeness of men.'[2] Divesting himself of his glory and majesty, Christ identified himself with man, entered his world and assumed human conditions. These conditions, moreover, were not graded to suit the person of God's Son; their harshness was not modified so that he could taste a little, but not too much, of the human lot, like a prince doing a few weeks in the armed forces to acquire a little insight into the life of the private soldier. On the contrary, Christ was to know the hard, unremitting toil of a Jewish peasant home. His birth was to be in the bareness of a stable, comparable perhaps in our time to birth in the broken-down dwelling of a refugee.

By isolating the Cross from the years leading up to Christ's public ministry, the whole significance of what Christ did is blunted and obscured. In order that the life of man could be restored and a new humanity inaugurated, that very same life, in all its harshness and limitations, had first of all to be assumed and borne. To achieve the purpose of God it was essential for Christ willingly to identify himself with the total life of man not merely as an experience from which he could opt out at any time but as a self-imposed condition from which, having undertaken it, there could be no escape but by the lonely portal of death—as it is for all other men; but

[1] John i. 14. [2] Phil. ii. 6-7.

because of his sinlessness and total obedience the very bonds of death which no man could break were, in Christ, broken for ever. The world and mankind could be redeemed only by one who entered fully and completely into its life and this is what the Incarnation stands for. If then we take the Incarnation as the first aspect of our Lord's life which the Church, his Body, must accept as a principle of his ministry, we are really saying that in its missionary task the Church too must identify itself with the world of men. In what ways can it do this? We might select four.

1. The Church to some extent carries out its task merely by being in the world. Many a parson has had the experience, when travelling by train, of seeing the door of the compartment open and a passenger about to enter and then, seeing the occupant, make a hasty retreat. This makes for comfortable travelling for the parson but it also seems to point to some disturbing element which his presence brings to people. It may be that some are allergic to the cloth or it may be that some are afraid that they will be involved in a long discussion about the state of their souls; but it could also be that the presence of the parson is a reminder of the eternal fact that man is called to a higher loyalty than himself; that man shall not live by bread alone; that there are standards of behaviour which man is called upon to follow; or it may be that it recalls some to the basic need for confession and pardon which every man needs. In some such way the very existence of the Church is a challenge to men and by its very presence it disturbs the life of the community. Like Christ it calls for an answer. Some men hated Christ because he made them face the fact of God: some men hate the Church because it too puts a question before them which they cannot permanently avoid answering. Life would be easier and more comfortable if the question were never raised: the existence of the Church,

even in its buildings, continually presents me with the need to make a reply.

II. The Church, like its Master, carries out its mission by preaching the Gospel. This is perhaps the most difficult of tasks today. It is one thing to preach within the four walls of the church, it is a rather different thing to preach outside in the open air. True, the great giants of the Evangelical Movement, Hywel Harris, Wesley, Whitfield, did this with tremendous results; and near our own time William Booth of the Salvation Army and Wilson Carlile of the Church Army did the same; but whether this is still the powerful weapon it used to be in a world of radio and television is open to question. The really important thing is that the Church should use whatever methods are available to communicate the Gospel and it may be that in this regard she is nothing like as effective as she ought to be.

III. The Church carries out its mission through the life and witness of its individual members. Wherever a Christian happens to be at any given time becomes the front line in the struggle between the Church and the world. It is here that the most effective missionary work is done and it is precisely at this point that many Christians not only fail in their witness but even believe that this side of their life is somehow not embraced by the Gospel: that real Christian work, as they sometimes call it, is only done within the context of the Church itself. In the Sunday School, the Youth Club, the Guild or the weekly meeting they step back from the world into the Christian milieu. Everyday occupations seem to some as unwarranted intrusions into this delightful and comfortable refuge in which the sound of hymns laps round them. This is the ghetto principle and this perhaps, more than anything else, needs to be reversed in the life of the Christian. It is the result of equating Christian witness with work within the orbit of the Church; it is described by that oft-quoted phrase 'a good church worker'. This is not to say that the Church has no need of such workers: its work would be impoverished without them; but it is essential to grasp that the Christian is also carrying on the mission of the Church when he is at his daily work or when he is engaged in trade union or civic affairs and that it is often here that the strain is greatest and the mission hardest. Here he or she often stands alone like a sentinel at the frontier of the Kingdom, exposed to all the dangers of such a position and without the moral support which a group of Christian people working together provides. We cannot perhaps do better than end with a quotation from Teilhard de Chardin in which he reinforces the plea of other Christian thinkers for what has been called 'worldly holiness' or 'secular sanctity'.[1]

Within the Church we observe all sorts of groups whose members are vowed to the perfect practice of this or that particular virtue: mercy, detachment, the splendour of the liturgy, the missions, contemplation. Why should there not be men vowed to the task of exemplifying, by their lives, the general sanctification of human endeavour? Men whose common religious ideal would be to give a full and conscious explanation of the divine possibilities or demands which any worldly occupation implies—men, in a word, who would devote themselves, in the fields of thought, art, industry, commerce and politics, etc., to carrying out in the sublime spirit these demands—the basic tasks which form the very bone-work of human society?

IV. The Church carries out its mission by identification with the needs of the world. This falls into two sections. First there are obviously many needs with which it is impossible to identify ourselves. For example it would be difficult for us to identify ourselves with the leper colonies of Africa and

[1] T. de Chardin, op. cit., p. 67.

India or with the refugees of Hong Kong. We may enter into their predicament through the use of our imagination but we cannot physically identify ourselves with their condition. All we can do is to provide what we can for the alleviation of their distress and to agitate in every way possible for action to be taken to terminate this state of things. We might call this identification through acts of charity, and the Christian Church has often—and still does—take a lead in this field. It has, through reformers like Wilberforce and Shaftesbury, changed the face of society and in Inter-Church Aid it has seen its obligation to shoulder the tragedy of those in want throughout the world.

But secondly there is the identification which demands the physical involvement of the Christian. Much of the overseas missionary work of the Church has meant this kind of identification: it has meant the physical presence of the missionary in alien surroundings; it has meant learning the language of the people to whom he goes; it has meant new habits and customs, as the more the missionary has identified himself with the life of the people, the better has he been able to carry out his task. This kind of identification is involved in all the great institutions which Christian compassion, reflecting the eternal compassion of God, has set in motion. In hospitals, in leprosaria, in institutions for the blind, the handicapped, or in moral welfare, it has been necessary for the Christian worker to put himself alongside those whom he has set out to help. It illustrates the incarnational principle that only by stepping down into the arena of human misery can human misery be alleviated. In its modern and most vivid form it can be seen in the figure of Kagawa of Japan, who lived in the Tokyo slums and embraced precisely the same conditions as those to whom he was sent—he never killed less than forty-five bedbugs in a night: or in the figure of

Father Loew, engaged in work among the dock workers of Marseilles, dining off the contents of a garbage pail; or in Father Damien, isolated with his lepers in the South Seas and slowly dying that they might have a chance to live.

Such are the ways by which the Church becomes identified with the world. It becomes enmeshed in the world and its needs, aspirations and tragedies. It does not forget that this is the divine method followed by the Master, who 'though he was rich, yet for your sakes he became poor, that ye through his poverty might be rich',[1] and a method which found its place in the most disturbing of all parables, the parable of the Great Surprise[2] as it has sometimes been called, in which the yardstick of our sincerity is our service of our brethren in distress.

B

Sufferings

Our Lord had to live in the world of men before he could redeem it. But he could not live as men live and be immune from the pressures which afflict all men as they face the world. We see this in the temptations which he endured: but we see it most clearly in the fact that the redemptive work of Christ involved weariness, hostility, opposition, criticism, resentment and misunderstanding both on the part of the disciples and on the part of the onlooker: and finally, on this path of the divine compassion, it meant the Cross.

The mission of the Church cannot be achieved without suffering. This should not surprise us, for Christ made it clear that he would suffer and that the life of the disciple would not be different from that of his Lord.[3] To some extent it might be argued that many Christians assume that the only

---

[1] 2 Cor. viii. 9.   [2] Matt. xxv. 31–46; Luke xxii. 27.
[3] Mark viii. 31; ix. 31; x. 33; Matt. x. 24; John xiii. 16 and xv. 20.

weapon which the Church requires is that of preaching. St. Paul certainly did not underestimate the power of preaching and neither should we; but he also knew and often drew attention to the need for suffering in the cause of Christ. To try and redeem the world merely by talking to it is to be unaware of the Gospel. The preaching and teaching of our Lord were one with his life and because they were so they brought him into collision with the powers of the world, and to defeat those powers meant the agony and suffering of the Cross. As one Christian writer has written: '. . . until Christ Crucified takes on visible form the world will not believe. "Except I shall see in His hands the print of the nails, and put my finger into the print of the nails . . . I will not believe!" This is precisely what the world says to the Church. We who talk of walking the way of the Cross dare not show men our hands: for we have not been wounded for them, we have not suffered for them. We have done little more than *preach* for them: and we cannot convince the world by our preaching of the Cross when we shrink from the Cross in our own lives.'[1] In plain practical terms this means that the Christian must apply his belief to his life; it will mean that he will see his possessions, his wealth, his talents, his time, his energy, as no longer his own but God's. It will mean that instead of spending in order to keep up with the proverbial Jones family, he will restrict his spending in order to give to some good cause; it will mean giving his time to some institution which desperately needs help; it will mean that he may feel compelled to enter the field of politics, a sphere from which too many Christians have withdrawn on the ground that 'politics is a dirty game'; he may long to be relieved of many of these duties but the knowledge that through his service the work of the Kingdom is somehow being done keeps him at his

[1] Bruce Kenrick, *The New Humanity* (1958), pp. 89–90.

station. Edmund Burke once said, 'All that is needed for the triumph of evil is that good men do nothing.' Far too long Christians have allowed evil to go unchecked because they have contracted out of the places where it can be stopped. Wherever the Christian witnesses, the Cross is carried and the sufferings are borne. Sometimes by disease and the sudden persecution which springs up against the Church death may come, but whether it be by this means or by the unremitting pressure of the modern world he enters into the sufferings of Christ.

III

We must now turn to the question: 'What is the relationship between the worship of the Church and the missionary task of the Church?' In the first place, worship is supremely important in the life of the Church because it is part of the rhythm of withdrawal and return. This is the recognition of the fact that, as the Scripture puts it, the Christian is 'in the world', he is not 'of the world'. Or as it is described in another New Testament phrase, we are a 'colony of heaven',[1] a nucleus of the new creation in enemy territory and need therefore to be constantly on our guard against conforming to this world or sliding quietly, almost imperceptibly into its ways until, without knowing it, we have lost sight of our true home. Worship is the means by which we are continually brought back to our true course. The world with its distractions and temptations always tends to make us loosen our hold on the real and eternal things; and we require this period of withdrawal from the world which worship provides, in order to be strengthened to return to the world to carry out the Church's mission.

[1] Phil. iii. 20: 'our citizenship (politeuma; R.V. marg, 'commonwealth') is in heaven', R.V.; 'we . . . are citizens of heaven', N.E.B.

Secondly, the worship of the Christian Church is made up of two parts: the Liturgy of the Word and the Liturgy of the Upper Room. The Communion Service of any church reveals this basic arrangement and it is a pattern which goes back to New Testament times. Every Lord's Day, for the first few centuries, this was the normal worship of the Christian Church. It is not possible here to go into the reasons why infrequent communion crept in, leaving the service in many traditions half-completed, or why the equally un-biblical habit arose of making communion an optional extra for the pious few who liked to remain at the end of the morning service. Our concern here must be to see how these two parts of the service are related to the mission of the church, in what way they serve to direct Christians to witness in the world.

The clue to this may be found in the term 'Liturgy of the Word'. The Word is the Word of God; it is God speaking to us. Just as through the centuries he spoke to his people through the prophets and finally in his Son, the *Word* made flesh, so he speaks to us today. The reading of the Scriptures gives us the historic context of our faith; it reminds us that our faith is rooted in history, not in legend; that it is a faith based on what God has done. But we do not read the Scriptures as ancient documents, interesting but remote and irrelevant; we go on to the exposition of them in the sermon, and the sermon makes these documents vehicles for a contemporary application, a word of the living God to his people now. The minister is the servant of the Word. This is symbolized in many traditions by the Little Entry; the congregation rises at the beginning of the service as the Bible is solemnly brought into church followed by the minister. The minister is not the servant of the congregation; he is not there to entertain, to provide what the congregation would like, or to deliver 'a little message' or to talk interestingly on some topic of the day, or to give his own views on a variety of things; he is there to preach God's word, not his own—and hence he often prefaces what he has to say with the words, 'In the name of the Father, the Son and the Holy Ghost'. This word of the living God is not necessarily a word of comfort. It can often be the real word to us when we find it most unpalatable, and perhaps one of the worst features of church life is the refusal of people to listen to what they do not want to hear. There is always the easy convenient way out, to go to another church where no challenge is issued, no demands made, and where possibly the biblical warning goes unheeded—'From the prophet even unto the priest everyone dealeth falsely, for they have healed the hurt of the daughter of my people lightly, saying Peace, peace; where there is no peace.'[1] The word of God is '... living and active, and sharper than any two edged sword, piercing even to the dividing of soul and spirit, of both joints and marrow, and quick to discern the thoughts and intents of the heart'.[2] One of the disciplines of the Christian life is to be exposed to the searching qualities of the Word; and it is not for nothing or purely for decorative purposes that many churches not only begin the service with the Bible being carried into the church, but that also during the service the Bible lies open on the Communion table, as a sign that we are continually subjected to its correction and continually directed by it to the needs of that world which the Church exists to serve.

Thirdly, the Church has, as part of its missionary task, the obligation to intercede for the world. Christ, the Ascended Lord, is also the Great High Priest who ever lives to make intercession for us. It is in this action of the Ascended Lord that the prayers of the Church for the needs of the world

[1] Jer. vi. 14; xviii. 11. [2] Heb. iv. 12.

ascend to the Father. Public worship as well as private prayer must have a place for intercession, and that intercession must be related to the events of the world in which we live. We need to use our imagination when we intercede, for we need to enter into the situation for which we are praying if we are to intercede intelligently, and we need to remember that our prayers, half-hearted as they so often are, enter into that great unbroken stream which ascends from every part of the world each day and find their home, through the upraised hands of the greater intercessor, in the heart of God.

The other half of the Christian pattern of worship is the Liturgy of the Upper Room or, as it is called in different traditions, the Lord's Supper, Holy Communion, the Eucharist or the Mass. In this part of the service man makes his response to God in thanksgiving. There are different traditions in the performance of this act of Christian worship but all traditions are recognizedly from the same sources and use, in varying degrees, the same material. It will be impossible to describe all the traditions here but by describing one of them the relation between it and the mission of the Church can be seen. The form selected is one of the best that the Reformed tradition has produced and it has widely influenced many other churches in their own liturgical revision. It is the service in the Church of Scotland *Book of Common Order* and the *Presbyterian Service Book*.

This tradition begins, as do so many others, with the so-called 'Comfortable Words'—'Come unto Me, all ye that labour and are heavy laden . . .'—and these words in themselves have a missionary significance for they are intended to strengthen as well as invite those who feel that they are not good enough to come to the Lord's Table. It is often stated that there are yet to be found in some of the remote Scottish islands men and women who, although attending church regularly, have never become communicant members. Their explanation is that they do not feel worthy enough to take such a step and at the Communion Service they are onlookers. While this is a very touching reminder of the solemnity of the occasion and one which the rest of us might sometimes recall when we take our religious obligations a little too lightly, it is nevertheless to lose sight of the redemptive purpose of God who, in Christ, came to 'seek and to save the lost'. If our salvation depended upon our worthiness, none of us could come to the Lord's Table, but the glory of it is that this is not so; our salvation depends on what God has done in Christ and it is for us humbly to receive it. These opening words describe God's attitude to the world. It is an attitude of mercy and compassion; it is the attitude of a Father who wishes to succour his children, and our acceptance of his compassion is the ground upon which we have the confidence to commend it to the world. It is at one and the same time both our encouragement to go out and the encouragement for those without to come in.

Next comes the Offertory. The Offertory is not merely the offerings of the faithful; it is also the bringing of the actual bread and wine. This is often called the Great Entry as distinct from the Little Entry at the beginning of the service. The bread and wine are brought into the church by representatives of the congregation and this offering of the elements symbolizes the giving to God of the whole of life. The bread is not simply a loaf; it represents the labour of the farmer who ploughed the field and sowed the seed; it represents the work of harvesting the corn and, in the case of wheat from overseas, its shipment to ports in our own land. Behind the loaf stand all the stages from the original planting of the seed to the docking of the ship, the purchase of the flour by the baker, the actual baking of the bread and its sale in the shop—a process involving all kinds of activity. Likewise the wine. These two represent and gather in themselves the life and labour of mankind; and in offering these to God the congregation is offering the whole life and work of its members to him.

This is an affirmation in visible form that the life and labour of mankind matter. It is an affirmation which springs from the scriptural view of the world as created by God and by a God who, having made it, did not spurn it but 'saw that it was very good'.[1] All this reinforces the vision of the world as the object of God's care and love and helps to destroy the false dichotomy between 'spiritual' and 'material' which has existed in widespread manner within the Church; a dichotomy which saw the Church as being responsible for 'spiritual things' while 'material things' were in some way inferior and fit only for the world and the worldly. It has been largely due to this baneful influence that the Church has contracted out of the world. By thinking of the world as a place from which to escape, the Church ceased to think of it as a place to transform. It is significant that where the Church has begun to see its task in a new light (as for example in many parishes influenced by the 'Parish and People' movement) the Great Entry has almost at once been introduced.[2]

After the offering of the gifts to the Father the Reformed liturgy turns to the Warrant. This is a term applied to the passage from St. Paul's First Epistle to the Corinthians[3] which gives an account of the tradition of the early Church. In Reformed practice it has always been necessary to have

[1] Gen. i. 31.

[2] It ought perhaps to be said that a large number of Scottish Parish Churches retained the Great Entry and were the only churches in the British Isles where this was to be seen. It was for this purpose that the well-loved tune 'St. George's, Edinburgh' was composed and the metrical version of the 24th Psalm set to that tune is still sung in very many churches as the Elders bring in the elements.

[3] I Cor. xi. 23–26.

scriptural warrant for what the Church does and this explains the term used for this passage and why it is read. The Church, over the centuries, has seen many promising movements come to nothing because they have ignored the sources from which the Church draws its strength and authority. One way of avoiding this as we embark on mission is to anchor what we do to Scripture. The Warrant having been read and the elements set apart the central section of the rite begins.

As has been said, the Liturgy of the Upper Room is the service in which man makes his response to God in Thanksgiving. The very name Eucharist means thanksgiving and the central part of the rite is known as the Eucharistic Prayer or Prayer of Thanksgiving. It commences with the 'Sursum Corda' or 'Lift up your hearts', the traditional introduction to the prayer, followed by 'the Preface' in which the congregation acknowledges that 'it is verily meet, right, and our bounden duty, that we should at all times and in all places *give thanks* . . .' to God the Creator who made man in his own image. Here is the acknowledgement of what man truly is and a reminder of that to which he is to be restored. This section ends with the Sanctus[1] and Benedictus,[2] as with angels and archangels and all the company of heaven we, the Church militant, join with the Church triumphant in ascribing all praise to God.

The Eucharistic Prayer then divides into three main parts. First there comes the Thanksgiving for our redemption in Christ and in this section the focal points of our Lord's life are mentioned: his incarnation, his perfect life on earth, his

---

[1] The Sanctus is: 'Holy, Holy, Holy, Lord God of Hosts,
    Heaven and earth are full of Thy glory:
    Glory be to Thee, O Lord Most High.'
[2] The Benedictus is: 'Blessed is He that cometh in the name of the Lord, Hosanna in the Highest.'

sufferings and death upon the Cross, his glorious resurrection and ascension, his continual intercession and rule at God's right hand. . . . We are, in this movement of the prayer, reminded not only of the cost of our redemption, our restoration to our new humanity, but we are reminded also of how it was achieved; and we see in this pattern the very pattern by which the Church of Christ, his Body, continues the task. Nothing could be more relevant to the Church's mission than this. Then with the pattern of our Lord's life before us, the Eucharistic prayer passes to its second phase in which, 'pleading His eternal sacrifice', the Church sets forth this memorial and asks that the Holy Spirit may be sent down upon both the people and their gifts so that, blessed by God, these elements may be, to those who receive in faith, the very body and blood of Christ. The third and final section is the self-offering of the whole congregation as the worshippers offer to God their souls and bodies to be 'a reasonable, holy and living sacrifice' and with this self-offering the offering also of their 'praise and thanksgiving': the self-offering of the congregation, the self-offering of the Church of God. One is tempted to ask just how far is the Church prepared to give itself so that the work of the Father may be done. Is it, for example, prepared to unite with other churches? Schemes have been put forward for union but too often churches seem to approach the proposition like two opponents in a ring slowly circling round each other in order to discover and exploit some weakness. The Church cannot be united on this basis, for this kind of approach means that one side is looking for victory over the other. What the churches need to learn is that the missionary task will require that they, as separate churches, shall die. The Church of Christ, the new humanity, cannot by its very nature be circumscribed by geographical or theological slant. The new humanity cannot be 'C. of E.',

Presbyterian, Methodist, Baptist or Congregationalist. The Church of today in a world in which all our problems are global must recover that primitive universality which belongs inherently to the 'new human'. To offer itself to God for use in his work is to offer itself to be an instrument of his will. This obedience which the Church as a body and in its individual members offers to its Lord must involve, if it be his will, the willingness to die that in his wisdom something new may arise.

The prayer ends with the traditional ascription of praise followed by the Lord's Prayer.

The reception of the elements follows. The congregation of Christian worshippers receives the bread and wine, symbols of the redemptive, atoning, reconciling work of Christ. As they receive them, they receive him and are united to him as branches of the one True Vine. As they receive, they feed on him who is the very Bread of Life. As they receive, sharing the bread and wine with their brethren, they also acknowledge their unity in Christ: 'For we being many are one bread, and one body: for we are all partakers of that one bread.'[1,2] As they receive they are also accepting, as part of the redemptive work of Christ, the sufferings which it may involve, for is it possible for any who take of the cup of salvation to fail to hear the words of the Master: 'Are ye able to drink of the cup that I shall drink of?',[3] or again, 'O my Father, if it be possible,' let this cup pass from me: nevertheless not as I will, but as thou wilt.'[4]

The elements having been received the minister gives the Pax or Peace in the words, 'The Peace of the Lord Jesus

---

[1] 1 Cor. x. 17.

[2] Many churches have the custom of passing round the loaf of bread and each member taking a piece of it. The Parish and People Movement has introduced this in many places.

[3] Matt. xx. 22.

[4] Matt. xxvi. 39.

Christ be with you all', a reminder of the first words uttered by the risen Lord to his disciples as they gathered together in Jerusalem: 'Peace be unto you.'[1] He then leads the people in a prayer of thanksgiving for the gift of the sacrament and concludes with the prayer of thanksgiving for the faithful departed—'the great cloud of witnesses by which we are compassed about'.[2]

The Church militant, engaged in the constant struggle with the forces of evil, is not simply an earthly institution battling against great odds, rather like a large welfare organization meeting once a week for the mutual edification of the members and listening to an address to boost morale. It is an earthly institution only in the sense that it is the visible and terrestrial manifestation of a body which is also heavenly. This has a profound effect on the mission of the Church; for it no longer appears as a task carried out in isolation or with a sense that no one knows or cares. On the contrary, Christians, as the writer of the Epistle to the Hebrews[3] puts it, are like people engaged in a struggle in the arena, around whose tiered sides are multitudes who have come to encourage them. These, for the Christian, are not idle spectators, but the 'cloud of witnesses' who, having fought the good fight themselves, stand within the heavenly host. For any Christian it must lighten the task to know that the invisible throng of saints is there to encourage him; for any worshipping community it must prove an inspiration to know that, concealed from us by the thinnest of veils, there is the continuous worship of the Church triumphant. The story is told of the saintly Bishop Westcott of Durham who was in the habit of worshipping each day in church. His daughter, knowing that hardly anyone else worshipped at that hour,

---

[1] Luke xxiv. 36; John xx. 21.   [2] Heb. xii. 1.
[3] Heb. xii. 1–12.

one day jestingly said to him on his return, 'Were there many there today, Father?', to which the old man replied, 'Yes, my dear, the church was full.' The Church is always full of the unseen cloud of witnesses: as the hymn has it, 'we feebly struggle, they in glory shine', but they only shine in glory because they once struggled, and we who now struggle may hope to come with them, if we are faithful to the end, to that glory which shines for ever.

The Benediction might, indeed, be more in tune with the intention of mission if it were to be in the form:

'Go forth into the world in peace; . . .'[1]

and some churches practise this. The elements are taken out of the church to the singing of a doxology or often to the words of the Nunc Dimittis—for in very truth our eyes have surely 'seen his salvation'.

Three comments may perhaps be made. First, nothing could be more obviously of the very stuff of mission than the Eucharist in which the self-offering of the congregation is made and the strength and unity of purpose is given to each person to be an agent of mission wherever God may place him. It has therefore often seemed strange to me that when some particular effort is required of a congregation or at the beginning of the year, a special 'service of dedication' has to be arranged. It raises the question, 'What does the Church think the Communion Service is?' The usual answer, if we are honest, is that the Communion Service is a piece of pious devotion strongly individualistic in tone and quite unconnected with the outward-looking role which the Church must

[1] The full text: 'Go forth into the world in peace; be of good courage; hold fast that which is good; render to no man evil for evil; strengthen the faint-hearted; support the weak; help the afflicted; honour all men; love and serve the Lord, rejoicing in the Holy Ghost. And the blessing of God Almighty, the Father, the Son and the Holy Spirit, be upon you, and remain with you for ever.'

always assume if it is to be true to its nature and purpose. It is not surprising that this state of affairs exists; for the way in which the Communion Service is related to the worship of the Church must inevitably make this so. To begin with, the so-called 'Free Churches' have infrequent Communion Services, once a quarter or at most once a month. There are historic reasons for this, but the position has been further weakened by the deplorable habit, also found in the Church of England, of making the Communion Service an optional extra tagged on at the end of the 'real service'. It is an amazing and almost unbelievable sight to see a host of people leave the church before the Communion begins while the minister sometimes dashes down to the front of the church to shake hands with them and generally see them off. How incredibly unbiblical a practice for churches which glory in the Bible! The Church of England is often little better. It is not unusual to find churches providing a number of Communion Services on a Sunday, so that everyone is catered for; and those who like to make their Communion at a time when no else is about, go early. How extraordinary that the great corporate act of the Church of God could be either an optional extra or so reduced to individualistic piety that its corporate aspect can be ignored in favour of a variety of occasions to suit the communicant. How can the Church see its task of missionary effort if religion is still presented in this subjective and individualist manner?

Secondly, the Communion Service is the Service of the Church. By this is meant that it is a corporate act and one which therefore ought to follow a prescribed order. There is a lot to be said for those members of the Established Church who complain of change in the services when the new incumbent arrives. They have a right to the form prescribed in the Book of Common Prayer without the private additions or unwarranted omissions of the 'High' churchman or the 'Low'. This situation is even worse in other churches where prescribed forms are regarded as anathema or as merely guides to the minister. The result of this state of affairs is a liturgical jungle in which all kinds of strange forms are used. Frequently the minister does what his predecessors did; or if he has views of his own he can make changes which have no rhyme or reason about them. Pieces of the Liturgy are left out; the sequence, if any, is often changed; occasionally irrelevant bits are put in because they are 'nice'.[1] This is an intolerable situation and the congregation suffers as a result of these purely personal approaches, often, if not always, made by men who have never taken the trouble to find out what the classical forms are. Whatever may be said against a prescribed form, it is certainly a protection for the congregation; and no man has the right to foist some concoction of his own upon his people if a first-class order, prescribed by the proper authorities of the Church, exists.

This leads to the final comment. The Liturgy, fully ordered, is the means by which God's people, over the years, enter into an understanding of the nature of the Church and of the meaning of the Christian life. This is not a new discovery. It is the basis of much of the Liturgical Movement; and some experts would argue that this movement began when, in 1909, Dom Lambert Beauduin addressed a Conference at Malines on these very lines. Beauduin, says Bouyer, saw that 'the liturgy itself, properly understood, is the fundamental catechesis of Christian doctrine, and that its presentation is the means most capable of stimulating and feeding the highest and purest spiritual life. . . . What pains priests take, he often thought, what labours they undergo to organize so many

[1] The failure to provide training in liturgical matters to those training for the Ministry is notorious.

works that are certainly useful, but of secondary importance!
But what would be the effects if priests took the same pains
to promote the rediscovery of essentials through a rediscovery
of the liturgy. . . .'[1]

It has often been borne out in experience that, given the
fully ordered Liturgy and the explanation of it, members of
the churches in the Reformed tradition have found an
entirely new meaning in the Communion Service, and one
has often been reproached with the words 'why haven't we
had this before?' Years and years of liturgical starvation have
often been the lot of too many of our people and yet, offered
the full order of service, they perceive that there is a richness
here which, though at the moment they cannot fully
apprehend it, is an opening out of new vistas of Christian
understanding which, bit by bit, they begin to make their
own. One illustration may suffice. The new minister introduced to his congregation the prayer of thanksgiving for the
faithful departed. Months elapsed and then one of his most
faithful members died suddenly: the following Sunday his
widow said to the minister, 'I often wondered why you used
that prayer for the faithful departed, now I know.' None of
us ever know fully the riches of Christ for they are unsearch-
able, but the worship of the Church should certainly be
comprehensive enough to lead us over the years into our
inheritance: and nothing does this more surely than the
Liturgy wherein, as has been said, 'elephants can swim and
lambs can wade'.[2]

---

[1] Louis Bouyer, *Life and Liturgy* (1956), pp. 59–60.
[2] Evelyn Underhill, *Worship*, 3rd edition (1937), p. 69.